Adam Smith

Series Introduction

The *Major Conservative and Libertarian Thinkers* series aims to show that there is a rigorous, scholarly tradition of social and political thought that may be broadly described as "conservative," "libertarian," or some combination of the two.

The series aims to show that conservatism is not simply a reaction against contemporary events, nor a privileging of intuitive thought over deductive reasoning; libertarianism is not simply an apology for unfettered capitalism or an attempt to justify a misguided atomistic concept of the individual. Rather, the thinkers in this series have developed coherent intellectual positions that are grounded in empirical reality and also founded upon serious philosophical reflection on the relationship between the individual and society, how the social institutions necessary for a free society are to be established and maintained, and the implications of the limits to human knowledge and certainty.

Each volume in the series presents a thinker's ideas in an accessible and cogent manner to provide an indispensable work for students with varying degrees of familiarity with the topic as well as more advanced scholars.

The following 20 volumes that make up the entire *Major Conservative and Libertarian Thinkers* series are written by international scholars and experts:

The Salamanca School by Andre Azevedo Alves (LSE, UK) and
   José Manuel Moreira (Universidade de Aveiro, Portugal)
Thomas Hobbes by R. E. R. Bunce (Cambridge, UK)
John Locke by Eric Mack (Tulane, UK)
David Hume by Christopher J. Berry (Glasgow, UK)
Adam Smith by James Otteson (Yeshiva, US)
Edmund Burke by Dennis O'Keeffe (Buckingham, UK)
Alexis de Tocqueville by Alan S Kahan (Paris, France)
Herbert Spencer by Alberto Mingardi (Istituto Bruno Leoni, Italy)
Ludwig von Mises by Richard Ebeling (Northwood, US)
Joseph A. Schumpeter by John Medearis (Riverside, California, US)
F. A. Hayek by Adam Tebble (UCL, UK)
Michael Oakeshott by Edmund Neill (Oxford, UK)
Karl Popper by Phil Parvin (Loughborough, UK)

Ayn Rand by Mimi Gladstein (Texas, US)
Milton Friedman by William Ruger (Texas State, US)
Russell Kirk by John Pafford (Northwood, US)
James M. Buchanan by John Meadowcroft (King's College London, UK)
The Modern Papacy by Samuel Gregg (Acton Institute, US)
Murray Rothbard by Gerard Casey (UCD, Ireland)
Robert Nozick by Ralf Bader (St Andrews, UK)

Of course, in any series of this nature, choices have to be made as to which thinkers to include and which to leave out. Two of the thinkers in the series—F. A. Hayek and James M. Buchanan—have written explicit statements rejecting the label "conservative." Similarly, other thinkers, such as David Hume and Karl Popper, may be more accurately described as classical liberals than either conservatives or libertarians. But these thinkers have been included because a full appreciation of this particular tradition of thought would be impossible without their inclusion; conservative and libertarian thought cannot be fully understood without some knowledge of the intellectual contributions of Hume, Hayek, Popper, and Buchanan, among others. While no list of conservative and libertarian thinkers can be perfect, then, it is hoped that the volumes in this series come as close as possible to providing a comprehensive account of the key contributors to this particular tradition.

John Meadowcroft
King's College London

Adam Smith

James R. Otteson

Major Conservative and
Libertarian Thinkers
Series Editor: John Meadowcroft
Volume 16

continuum

2011

The Continuum International Publishing Group
80 Maiden Lane, New York, NY 10038
The Tower Building, 11 York Road, London SE1 7NX

www.continuumbooks.com

Library of Congress Cataloging-in-Publication Data
Otteson, James R.
Adam Smith/James R. Otteson.
p. cm. – (Major conservative and libertarian thinkers)
Includes bibliographical references and index.
ISBN-13: 978-0-8264-2983-4 (hardcover: alk. paper)
ISBN-10: 0-8264-2983-1 (hardcover: alk. paper)
1. Smith, Adam, 1723-1790. 2. Classical school of economics.
3. Free enterprise. I. Title. II. Series.

HB103.S6O88 2010
330.15'3082–dc22   2010022007

ISBN: HB: 978-0-8264-2983-4

Typeset by Newgen Imaging Systems Pvt Ltd, Chennai, India
Printed and bound in the United States of America by Thomson-Shore, Inc

To George
Who Brings Such Joy to Life

Contents

Series Editor's Preface

Adam Smith is popularly believed to have been a crude defender of free market capitalism; his name is often associated with the idea that the "invisible hand" of the market will guide people to beneficent outcomes *as if by magic* if market forces are left to operate unhindered. However, as Professor James R. Otteson of Yeshiva University sets out in this book, Smith was in fact an extremely subtle and sophisticated thinker who made important and lasting contributions to the disciplines of economics, politics, law, philosophy, and ethics. These contributions can be found in particular in the two books Smith published during his lifetime, *The Theory of Moral Sentiments* and *An Enquiry into the Nature and Causes of the Wealth of Nations* that are the principal focus of this book.

In the context of a discussion of international trade, Smith did indeed write in *The Wealth of Nations* that in certain circumstances an individual pursuing his own self-interest would be "led by an invisible hand to promote an end that was no part of his intention." But, as Otteson explains, this was not a statement of blind faith in the free market, but part of a careful exposition of the counter-intuitive notion that beneficent outcomes are very often not the result of deliberate planning, but rather arise spontaneously as an unintended consequence of actions directed toward other ends. Hence, tradespeople who enter the marketplace seeking only their own gain provide goods and services for others and by so doing contribute to the creation of the broader institutional framework of an advanced market economy that is the basis of prosperity and thus the wealth of nations.

Smith's contribution to conservative and libertarian thought is most apparent and acute in this appreciation of the fundamentally spontaneous nature of social order and the destructive potential of attempts to deliberately plan that order. Smith is part of a tradition of political economy that is skeptical of the ability of politicians to improve upon the outcomes generated spontaneously by the market. In this regard his work was an important precursor of later conservative and libertarian thinkers whose ideas are also presented in this series, notably Hayek, Buchanan, and Friedman.

This volume makes a crucial contribution to the *Major Conservative and Libertarian Thinkers* series by presenting Smith's thought in an accessible and cogent form. It is an outstanding work that provides a thorough account of Smith's life and work, and then considers Smith's enduring significance in terms of what Smith got wrong and what Smith got right. It is a book that will prove indispensable to those unfamiliar with Smith's work as well as more advanced scholars.

John Meadowcroft
King's College London

Preface

This book is a part of a series entitled "Major Conservative and Libertarian Thinkers." The series aims to introduce these thinkers to a wider audience, providing an overview of their lives and works, as well as expert commentary on their enduring significance. Thus *Adam Smith* begins with a short biography of Smith; it then gives an overview and discussion of his extant works, focusing on his two major publications, the 1759 *Theory of Moral Sentiments* and the 1776 *Wealth of Nations*; and it concludes by discussing what Smith got right, what he got wrong, and why he is still worth reading—which he most definitely is. Also included is a bibliography of primary and secondary sources.

A slim volume like this can address only a fraction of the richness of Smith's work, so it can be only a primer. One principle that has helped guide my selection of topics has been the aim of the book's series.[1] Thus I have given added weight, where appropriate, to aspects of Smith's thought that justify, or at least explain, his inclusion in a series about major conservative and libertarian thinkers. Depending on how one defines those terms, there are aspects of Smith's thought that are conservative and aspects that are libertarian; and there are aspects that are neither.

I also try to make sense of Smith's writing not only in the small but in the large as well—that is, not only in the details of this or that argument in this or that work, but in the larger aims of Smith's scholarly corpus. I believe there is a coherence to Smith's work, and, though I realize a book like this places limits on an attempt to demonstrate a claim like that, I do my best to make it plausible if not ultimately convincing.

In writing the book I have been conscious that for some readers it might serve as their first introduction to Smith, and for others it might serve as their only introduction to him. For a thinker as important as Smith, that makes the stakes for a book like this one high indeed. I have striven to present Smith in a

Preface

way I believe he himself would have approved: charitably but objectively. No author, however brilliant, got everything right, so the reader will also find in these pages periodic discussion of problems or objections, as well as indications of ongoing scholarly criticism or debate. But I believe that some important aspects of Smith's contributions endure, and I hope that by the end of this book you are convinced of that as well.

The best way to understand Smith remains, and will always remain, reading his works for oneself. If this book gives you reason to think that you should read Smith, it will have served its primary purpose.

Notes

[1] This is especially important given that some scholars—for example Brubaker (2006)—argue that Smith is "neither a conservative nor a libertarian," while others—McLean (2006), for example—claim that Smith is a "radical egalitarian."

Acknowledgments

Only a short time ago I would not have imagined that I would write another book about Adam Smith. Thanks must therefore go to John Meadowcroft, general editor of the series "Major Conservative and Libertarian Thinkers" for Continuum Press, for convincing me to do so. He must also be thanked for his dogged persistence, as well as his patience.

I would also like to thank students at the University of Alabama, at Georgetown University, and at Yeshiva University who have read Smith with me and have patiently considered my arguments about what makes Smith so interesting and important. Similarly, I thank the many conferees at Liberty Fund colloquia over the years who have helped shape my understanding of Smith. I also thank Liberty Fund itself for making these colloquia possible.

Special thanks goes to Max Hocutt, for helping me understand ethical theory (and so much else); to Bradley Birzer, for helping me understand what charitable scholarship is and for continually reminding me to focus on what is truly important; and to Steven Grosby, for helping me understand what honorable and civilized collegiality is. These three also provide continuing and inspiring models of friendship in the high tradition of Aristotle and Cicero.

Finally, I thank my beloved family—Katharine, Victoria, James, Joseph, and George—for their patience, love, and support. In this, as in everything else, they are the *sine qua non*.

List of Abbreviations

The now standard edition of Smith's works is the Glasgow Edition of the *Works and Correspondence of Adam Smith,* published in cloth by Oxford University Press and in paper by Liberty Fund. I use this edition of Smith's works throughout, with the following abbreviations:

C	*Correspondence of Adam Smith*
EPS	*Essays on Philosophical Subjects*
HA	"The Principles which Lead and Direct Philosophical Enquiries; Illustrated by the History of Astronomy" (reprinted in EPS)
HAP	"The Principles which Lead and Direct Philosophical Enquiries; Illustrated by the History of Ancient Physics" (reprinted in EPS)
"Languages"	"Considerations Concerning the First Formation of Languages, and the Different Genius of Original and Compounded Languages" (reprinted in LRBL)
LJ	*Lectures on Jurisprudence*
LRBL	*Lectures on Rhetoric and Belles Lettres*
TMS	*The Theory of Moral Sentiments*
WN	*An Inquiry into the Nature and Causes of the Wealth of Nations*

Smith's works are also available at the Liberty Fund's Online Library of Liberty, here: http://oll.libertyfund.org/index. php?option=com_staticxt&staticfile=show.php&title=197. The Online Library of Liberty is indexed and searchable, and it provides facsimiles as well as other formats.

Part I

Biography

Chapter 1

Adam Smith's Life and Works

In the Beginning

Adam Smith was born in 1723 in Kirkcaldy, Scotland, and died in Edinburgh in 1790. Along with figures like his teacher Francis Hutcheson (1694–1746) and his friend David Hume (1711–76), Smith was one of the principals of a period of astonishing learning that has become known as the Scottish Enlightenment. He is the author of two published books: the 1759 *Theory of Moral Sentiments* (TMS) and the 1776 *Inquiry into the Nature and Causes of the Wealth of Nations* (WN). TMS brought Smith considerable acclaim during his lifetime and was soon considered one of the great works of moral theory—impressing, for example, such luminaries as Immanuel Kant (1724–1804), who called Smith his "*Liebling*" or "favorite," and Charles Darwin (1809–82), who in his 1871 *Descent of Man* endorsed and accepted several of Smith's "striking" conclusions. TMS went through fully six revised editions during Smith's lifetime. Yet since the nineteenth century, Smith's fame has largely rested on his second book, which, whether judged by its influence or its greatness, must be considered one of the most important works of the second millennium.

Not many details of Smith's boyhood are known. He was born on the 5th of June and was an only child, his father, also named Adam Smith, having died shortly before he was born. In his 1793 *Account of the Life and Writings of Adam Smith, LL.D.*, Smith's student Dugald Stewart reports that Smith's "constitution during infancy was infirm and sickly, and required all the tender solicitude of his surviving parent. She was blamed for treating him with an unlimited indulgence; but it produced no unfavourable effects on his temper or his dispositions" (EPS, 269). Perhaps one anecdote from Smith's childhood bears repeating. Margaret, Smith's mother, would regularly take him to Strathenry, about seven miles northwest of Kirkaldy, to visit her brother, Smith's uncle. On one visit, when the wee Smith was but 3 years old, he was playing in front of his uncle's house and was kidnapped by a passing group of gypsies. The alarm was raised and the gypsies were discovered and overtaken in the nearby Leslie wood, whereupon the wailing toddler was safely returned to his family. Stewart writes that Smith's uncle, who recovered Smith, "was the happy instrument of preserving to the world a genius, which was destined, not only to extend the boundaries of science, but to enlighten and reform the commercial policy of Europe" (EPS, 270). In his 1895 *Life of Adam Smith,* John Rae notes dryly, "He would have made, I fear, a poor gipsy" (LAS, 5).

Smith matriculated at the University of Glasgow in 1737 at the age of 14. His instruction there, which was heavy in the classics, Smith considered quite good; the influence of Hutcheson, to whom Smith later referred as "the never to be forgotten Dr Hutcheson" (C, 309), was pronounced. After Glasgow, Smith was elected as a Snell exhibitioner at Balliol College, Oxford. Smith was not so impressed with the quality of instruction at Oxford: "In the university of Oxford, the greater part of the public professors have, for these many years, given up altogether even the pretence of teaching" (WN V.i.f.8).[1] Smith was able to make good use of the libraries at Oxford, however, studying widely in English, French, Greek, and Latin literature. He left Oxford and returned to Kirkaldy in 1746.

In 1748, at the invitation of Henry Home, Lord Kames (1696–1782), Smith began giving in Edinburgh "Lectures on Rhetoric and the *Belles Lettres,*" as Kames's biographer Alexander Tytler reports, focusing on literary criticism and the arts of speaking and writing well. It was during this time that Smith met and befriended David Hume, who was to become Smith's closest confidant and greatest philosophical influence. Smith left Edinburgh to become Professor of Logic at the University of Glasgow in 1751 and then Professor of Moral Philosophy there in 1752. The lectures he gave at Glasgow eventually crystallized into TMS, first published in 1759.

Smith's First Book: TMS

In TMS, Smith argues that human beings naturally desire a "mutual sympathy of sentiments" with their fellows, which means that they long to see their own judgments and sentiments echoed in others. Because we all seek out this "sympathy" (TMS I.i.2.1)[2]—or "harmony" or "concord" of sentiments—much of social life is a give-and-take whereby people alternately try to moderate their own sentiments so that others can "enter into them" and try to arouse others' sentiments so that they match their own. This process of mutual adjustment results in the gradual development of shared habits, and then rules, of judgment about matters ranging from etiquette to moral duty. This process also gives rise, Smith argues, to an ultimate standard of moral judgment, the "impartial spectator," whose imagined perspective we use to judge both our own and others' conduct. When we use it to judge our own, it constitutes our conscience. We consult the impartial spectator simply by asking ourselves what a fully informed but disinterested person would think about our conduct. If such a person would approve, then we may proceed; if he would disapprove, then we should desist. If we heed the impartial spectator, then we feel a pleasurable satisfaction, which reinforces our behavior; by contrast, if we disobey, then we feel an unpleasant guilt, which provides a disincentive for the behavior.

Morality on Smith's account is thus an earthly, grounded affair. Although Smith makes frequent reference to God and the "Author of Nature," scholars disagree over to what extent such references do any real work in his theory—and thus to what extent Smith's theory of moral sentiments is a relativistic account, eschewing reliance on transcendent, objective rules of morality. We take this issue up in Chapters 3 and 4.

One important concern with Smith's moral theory will be the extent to which Smith is merely *describing* the phenomenon of human morality, as a natural scientist or anthropologist might, or whether he is also making moral *endorsements*, as a person concerned to help people lead good or righteous lives might. Smith is doing at least the former: one of his central goals is to describe the origins, maintenance, and development of the human social institution of commonly shared morality. But is he also making or recommending moral judgments? Students of TMS disagree about this. I will argue that Smith is offering a hypothetical imperative: given your nature and given the nature of human social institutions, your best chance of being happy is to follow, at least for the most part, your community's moral traditions.

Interregnum: between TMS and WN

In 1763 Smith resigned his post at Glasgow to become the personal tutor of Henry Scott, the Third Duke of Buccleuch, whom Smith then accompanied on an 18-month tour of France and Switzerland. It was during these travels with the Duke that Smith met the French *philosophe* Voltaire (1694–1778), on whom Smith apparently made quite an impression: Voltaire later wrote, "This Smith is an excellent man! We have nothing to compare with him, and I am embarrassed for my dear compatriots" (Muller 1993: 15). During these travels Smith also met François Quesnay (1694–1774), Jacques Turgot (1727–81), and others among the so-called French Physiocrats, who were arguing for a relaxation of trade barriers and generally laissez-faire economic policies. Although Smith had already been developing his own similar ideas, conversations with the Physiocrats no doubt helped him refine and sharpen them. In 1767, Smith returned to Kirkcaldy to care for his ailing mother and to continue work on what would become his WN. During that time he was supported by a generous pension from the Duke of Buccleuch, enabling him to focus on his scholarly work. It was known that the celebrated author of TMS was working furiously on a new book, and the 10 years he labored on it raised expectations high indeed. Finally, at long last, Smith's magnum opus was published March 9, 1776.

The reactions to the publication of WN were swift and, among the principals of the Scottish Enlightenment at least, highly laudatory. Here is Hume's reaction:

> Euge! Belle! Dear Mr. Smith: I am much pleas'd with your Performance, and the Perusal of it has taken me from a State of great Anxiety. It was a Work of so much Expectation, by yourself, by your Friends, and by the Public, that I trembled for its Appearance; but am now much relieved. Not but that the Reading of it necessarily requires so much Attention, and the Public is disposed to give so little, that I shall still doubt for some time of its being very popular: But it has Depth and Solidity and Acuteness, and is so much illustrated by curious Facts, that it must at last take the public Attention. (C, 150)

Here is Hugh Blair (1718–1800), Moderator of the General Assembly of the Church of Scotland and Professor of Rhetoric at the University of Edinburgh: "You have given me full and Compleat Satisfaction and my Faith is fixed. I do think the Age is highly indebted to you, and I wish they may be duly Sensible of the Obligation" (C, 151). William Robertson (1721–93), eminent historian and Principal of the University of Edinburgh: "You have formed into a regular and consistent system one of the most intricate and important parts of political science, and [. . .] I should think your Book will occasion a total change in several important articles in police and finance" (C, 153). And Adam Ferguson (1723–1816), Professor of Moral Philosophy at the University of Edinburgh and author of the 1767 *Essay on the History of Civil Society*: "You are surely to reign alone on these subjects, to form the opinions, and I hope to govern at least the coming generations" (C, 154). Somewhat later, Thomas Malthus (1766–1834), author of *An Essay on the Principle of Population*, went so far as to claim that Smith's WN "has done for political economy, what the *Principia* of Newton did for physics" (1986: 257).

Smith's Second Book: WN

In WN, Smith argues, against the school of economic thought called Mercantilism, that real wealth does not consist in pieces of metal: it consists rather in the relative ability to satisfy one's needs and desires. Since each person always wishes to "better his own condition" (see, for example, WN II.iii.31), the argument of WN is that those policies and public institutions should be adopted that best allow each of us to do so. Hence the task of the political economist is to conduct empirical, historical investigations to discover what these policies and institutions are. His own investigation led Smith to argue that markets, in which the division of labor is allowed to progress, in which trade is free, and in which taxes and regulations are light, are the most conducive to this end. Smith argues that in market-oriented economies based on private property, each person working to better his own condition will increase the supply, and thus lower the price, of whatever good he is producing; this means that others will in turn be a better position to afford his goods. Thus each person serving his own ends is led, in Smith's famous phrase, "by an invisible hand" (WN IV.ii.9) simultaneously to serve everyone else's ends as well, both by providing more plentiful and a greater diversity of goods and by thereby lowering prices. The market, Smith believed, could harness people's industry in the service of their own ends and make it serve everyone else's welfare, even if the welfare of others was not part of the individuals' own motivations.

Smith did not think that everyone is fundamentally selfish in any narrow sense. In opposition to Bernard Mandeville (1670–1733), whose 1714 *Fable of the Bees* Smith called "licentious," Smith argued that people's "self-interest" in fact includes the interests of others, in particular their family and friends, even their country or countrymen. Nevertheless Smith did believe that natural benevolence is limited and that, whatever other motivations people feel, their desire to better their own conditions is always present. Thus "It is not from the benevolence of the butcher, the brewer, or the baker, that we expect our dinner, but from their regard to their own interest" (WN I.ii.2). The genius of the Smithian market mechanism was that it could coordinate the disparate individual efforts of indefinitely many persons and derive an overall benefit for the good of society from them.

The conclusions of WN are therefore largely in favor of limiting political interference in markets. Each individual knows his own situation—including his goals and desires, as well as the opportunities available to him—better than anyone else does, and certainly better than any distant legislator. Hence Smith argues that individuals themselves should be allowed to decide how best to apply and sell their labor or goods, with whom to trade and on what terms, and so on. Smith is withering in his condemnation of meddling legislators who overestimate their ability to direct the lives of others, who legislatively substitute their own distant judgment for that of the individuals with actual local knowledge over whom they rule, and who then use the predictable failures of their decisions as excuses for yet more imprudent intervention.

Yet Smith is equally condemnatory of grasping merchants and businessmen who seek legal protections of their industries or prices. "People of the same trade seldom meet together," Smith writes, "even for merriment and diversion, but the conversation ends in a conspiracy against the publick, or in some contrivance to raise prices" (WN I.x.c.27). Such merchants proclaim that trade barriers, tariffs, and other legal protections are for the good of the country, but Smith exposes these claims as special pleading, since they work to increase those particular merchants' profits at the expense not only of their competitors but also of the public at large. Keeping prices up and limiting competition will certainly benefit the favored businessmen, but such policies just as certainly impose artificial costs on everyone else. Smith argues that the way to deal with such attempts at legalized monopoly is typically not to regulate them, however, but rather to disallow legally enforced privileges in the first place. Markets and open competition are, Smith thinks, better providers of social benefit than short-sighted regulation by politically motivated legislators—who are, after all, often remunerated handsomely by the very merchants and businesses from whom they profess to protect the public.

But Smith is no anti-government anarchist, nor even a modern-day libertarian. He argues that the first and central duty of the government is to secure "justice," which for him means protecting people's lives, property, and voluntary contracts. This will entail a system of police and courts, which Smith argues must be effective and efficient if the market system is going to be able to work. In addition to those basic duties, however, Smith also argues that the government should provide out of general taxation for those goods that would conduce to everyone's benefit but that would not repay any private entrepreneurs to provide. In this category he suggests the building of roads, canals, and other public infrastructures. He recommends moreover partially state-subsidizing primary schooling, in the belief that everyone should learn to "read, write, and account" (WN V.i.f.54).

But his concerns for the common man go far deeper. Indeed, one of Smith's central concerns is those at the low end of the economic scale. This concern is especially pronounced in book 5 of WN, where Smith worried about the deleterious effects on workers' minds that the progressing division of labor would have. "The man whose whole life is spent in performing a few simple operations," he writes,

> of which the effects too are, perhaps, always the same, or very nearly the same, has no occasion to exert his understanding, or to exercise his invention in finding out expedients for removing difficulties which never occur. He naturally loses, therefore, the habit of such exertion, and generally becomes as stupid and ignorant as it is possible for a human creature to become. (WN V.i.f.50)

So although markets and division of labor provide great material benefits, Smith also believed they can deaden the mind and
weaken the character. Nationally subsidized schooling might
help, but it is not clear that Smith thought this would be enough.
Indeed, some recent commentators have suggested that Smith's
deep concern for the poor and working portions of society
in fact make him rather a precursor to modern "progressive"
liberalism than an icon of classical laissez-faire liberalism.

By the middle of the nineteenth century, WN was regularly
cited in British parliament—in debates about its Corn Laws, for
example—and its recommendations of free markets and free
trade went on to have great influence in the subsequent political
and economic developments not only of Britain, but also of most
of the Western and even parts of the Eastern world. Smith's
influence on the founding of the United States in particular was
also pronounced. Among his readers were Benjamin Franklin
(1706–90), George Washington (1732–99), Thomas Paine
(1737–1809), and Thomas Jefferson (1743–1826). When com-
piling "a course of reading" in 1799, Jefferson included WN
along with John Locke's 1690 *Second Treatise of Government* and
Condorcet's 1793 *Esquisse d'un tableau des progrès de l'esprit humain*
as the essential books (Rothschild 2001: 4). The English historian Henry Thomas Buckle (1821–62) wrote that WN "is probably the most important book that has ever been written,"
including the Bible (Skousen 2001: 20). Today many countries
in the world either rely on some version of Smithian market-
based economies or are in the process of creating them.

After WN

Smith remained in Kirkcaldy until 1778, when he became
Commissioner of Customs in Edinburgh. Smith's mother died
in 1784, when Smith was aged 61. Smith had spent much of this
time caring for his mother, which might be part of the explanation for the fact that he never married or had children. Although
he apparently did have a love interest during his adult life, it did
not result in marriage. Dugald Stewart writes,

> In the early part of Mr Smith's life it is well known that he was
> for several years attached to a young lady of great beauty and

accomplishment. How far his addresses were favourably received, or what the circumstances were which prevented their union, I have not been able to learn; but I believe it is pretty certain that, after this disappointment, he laid aside all thoughts of marriage. The lady to whom I allude died also unmarried. (EPS, 349–50)

During the decade or so that he spent in Kirkcaldy, and then thereafter when he was in Edinburgh, Smith spent a great deal of time visiting with and entertaining friends, among whom he counted Irish Catholic philosopher and statesman Edmund Burke (1729–97), the chemist Joseph Black (1728–99), the geologist James Hutton (1726–97), Prime Minister Frederick (Lord) North (1732–92), and Prime Minister William Pitt the Younger (1759–1806). He also took active roles in learned organizations like the Oyster Club, the Poker Club, and the Select Society, the last of which including among its members William Robertson, David Hume, James Burnett Lord Monboddo (1714–99), Adam Ferguson, and Lord Kames.[3] In 1783, Smith was a founding member of the Royal Society of Edinburgh, which exists still today as Scotland's premier national academy of science and letters. Having previously served as the University of Glasgow's Dean of Arts (1760) and Vice-Rector (1761–63), in 1787 he was elected Lord Rector of the university, a post he held until 1789.

During his years in Edinburgh, Smith extensively revised both TMS and WN for new editions. He reported to Le Duc de La Rochefoucauld in 1785 that during this time

I [Smith] have likewise two other great works upon the anvil; the one is a sort of Philosophical History of all the different branches of Literature, of Philosophy, Poetry and Eloquence; the other is a sort of theory and History of Law and Government. (C, 248)

Neither of these projects was ever published. In the days before he died, Smith summoned Black and Hutton to his quarters and asked that they burn his unpublished manuscripts, a request they had resisted on previous occasions. This time Smith insisted. They reluctantly complied, destroying 16 volumes of manuscripts. It is probable that Smith's philosophical history of literature, philosophy, poetry, and eloquence and his theory and history of law and government were among the works that perished in that tragic loss.

Adam Smith died in Edinburgh on July 17, 1790, and is buried in the Canongate cemetery off High Street in Edinburgh. His grave marker reads:

HERE

ARE DEPOSITED

THE REMAINS OF

ADAM SMITH.

AUTHOR

OF THE

THEORY OF MORAL SENTIMENTS,

AND

WEALTH OF NATIONS:

ETC. ETC. ETC.

HE WAS BORN 5TH JUNE 1723

AND HE DIED 17TH JULY 1790

Notes

[1] I use the now standard notation in referring to passages in Smith's WN and TMS: "WN V.i.f.8" means *Wealth of Nations,* book V, chapter i, article f, paragraph 8.

[2] This notation means *Theory of Moral Sentiments,* part I, section i, chapter 2, paragraph 1.

[3] For an overview of these groups and their memberships, see Broadie (2001).

Part II

Ideas

Chapter 2

Smith's Philosophical Program
Two Early Essays

Early in his scholarly career, Smith wrote a short essay entitled "Considerations Concerning the First Formation of Languages, and the Different Genius of Original and Compounded Languages" (LRBL, 203–26). Today almost no one other than scholars knows about the essay, but Smith himself thought quite highly of it, insisting that the second and all subsequent editions of his *Theory of Moral Sentiments* (TMS) during his lifetime have this essay appended to it. What was it about the essay that so appealed to Smith? This little essay offers a foreshadowing of things to come: It exhibits the philosophical method Smith would develop and employ in his subsequent work, a method that would become emblematic of the "Scottish Historical School" of social thought.[1] And it gives an early indication of some of the central principles Smith believed were at work in human social institutions.

Smith's "Languages"

Smith begins this short essay by referring to a hypothetical state of nature:

> Two savages, who had never been taught to speak, but had been bred up remote from the societies of men, would naturally begin to form that language by which they would endeavour to make their mutual wants intelligible to each other. (LRBL 203, §1)

Their first words would be proper names referring to objects with which they had most experience and were thus most familiar; as their "more enlarged experience" revealed other instances of similar objects, the proper names would become common nouns (ibid.). So what was first called Cave, Tree, and Fountain (Smith's examples) would come to be known as a cave, a tree, and a fountain, these terms now applied to other objects that resemble the original templates (LRBL 204–5, §2). Smith then explains how other kinds of words—adjectives, prepositions, then verbs—also arise in response to early humans' felt needs and their localized experiences.

The development of language, according to Smith, is a process with several interesting features. First, it has no prior existence: it is a human creation, not a human discovery. On Smith's telling, language develops and changes in response to individuals' needs, and the rules of usage, pronunciation, and diction also arise, develop, and change according to the needs of the language users. Note that this does not mean there are no rules, only that the rules are more like the rules of baseball than the laws of physics: without humans there are no rules of baseball, but the laws of physics exist regardless. So in a state of nature humans would have needs, and they would discover, through trial and error, that communicating those desires in language is a more effective way of satisfying their desires than, say, using merely hand signals. But language would only be useful if the meanings of words and sentences were relatively stable and commonly understood. If you and I attached different meanings to the same word, or if we changed the words' meanings in unpredictable ways from one usage to the next, then our attempts to "make our mutual wants intelligible to each other" would be frustrated. Thus there is a natural incentive not only to develop an increasingly complex system of language that matches our increasingly complex world, but also to work toward settled and known rules of usage. Further trial and error and further "enlarged experience" will encourage further development of language, but to serve its reason for being language will need a recognized framework that at any given time is relatively stable.

Another important feature of language, according to Smith, is that its development takes place "insensibly and by such slow degrees" that speakers "are scarce ever sensible" of the changes (LRBL 220, §33). This may seem a paradoxical claim: Since the speakers are the ones making the changes, shouldn't they be aware of them? The answer is that they may be locally, but not globally, aware—another perhaps paradoxical claim, but one that becomes centrally important to the rest of Smith's work. Smith's idea is that speakers for the most part have only local intentions: they have this desire, which they wish to communicate now, to this audience. Because human experience is constantly changing, people's purposes, circumstances, and interlocutors also change. So new words, usages, or pronunciations develop in response to new situations whose particulars gave rise to individuals' felt need to innovate. Language entrepreneurs try out new ways of expressing themselves in order to achieve their purposes, whatever they are. According to Smith, most new usages are based on previous, settled usages, but some may be entirely new. Most do not catch on, but some will if they satisfy a need or purpose of other speakers as well. At the local level, then, language is sometimes turbulent and under construction. At a higher level, order arises, but it is an "unintentional order" because no one specifically intended it. As Smith puts it, new usages "would happen without any intention or foresight in those who first set the example, and who never meant to establish any general rule. The general rule would establish itself insensibly, and by slow degrees" (LRBL 211, §16).

The Rules of Language and Spontaneous Order

The rules of language, then, are conventions that we learn to follow mostly without realizing it and mostly by habit. Sometimes the rules get written down, but grammar books and dictionaries are not themselves the sources of the rules. They can only record previously settled de facto rules—which is why they quickly become dated. Like the rules of baseball, they are created by humans, and they arose piecemeal and in response to localized needs. If you read today's *Handbook of Official Rules for Major League Baseball*,[2] you might get the impression that some very smart people sat down, conceived the whole thing, and, as it were, gave birth to the full system of rules like Athena from Zeus's head. But a look at, for example, the history of the Strike Zone[3] will quickly disabuse you of that notion: it has undergone repeated substantial changes over baseball's history, each emendation a result of trial-and-error experience. In other words, the rules were changed to better accommodate baseball players' (and fans') desires, which themselves also undergo change over time. Contrast that with the laws of physics. Scientists have certainly changed their minds many times about what those laws are. Think even of the changes from the time of Newton, whom Smith considered to have set the standard for philosophical— what we today would call "scientific"—researches, to the time of Einstein. The difference between changes in scientific theories and those in the rules of language, however, is that the former are successive attempts to comprehend and describe an external reality, a reality whose nature, it is usually held, does not change. So science is the progressive attempt to develop new or better ways to capture and represent an external reality, and the regularities that scientists describe they have discovered, not invented. Hence whereas baseball and language are entirely dependent on human needs, desires, and actions, the laws of behavior of physical objects have an existence independent of humans.[4]

The upshot, to return to Smith, is that on his account language is an example of what has come to be called "spontaneous order": a system of order that is, to paraphrase Smith's contemporary Adam Ferguson,[5] the result of human action but not of human design. An example will illustrate. Consider the word "brethren": in the eighteenth century, "brethren" was a commonly used form for the plural of "brother"; "brothers" had not yet taken over as the preferred form. Smith uses both forms, with a slight preference for "brethren."[6] Yet in the over two centuries since Smith wrote, "brothers" has almost totally crowded "brethren" out as the preferred term. The analysis Smith gives in "Languages" would explain this transition as the result of millions of decisions individual English speakers made over that time that gradually shifted the preference. The change was probably so gradual that few will have noticed it, and fewer still will have deliberately altered their speech either to reflect the change or to initiate it. People's deliberate intentions were instead focused on their nearer goals: communicating idea X to person A at time T. Nevertheless their usages gave rise to a larger pattern of order that is observable. In the eighteenth century, the rule regarding the forming the plural of "brother" would probably have been something like, "The plural of 'brother' is either 'brethren' (preferred) or 'brothers.'" By contrast, the rule today, which most could probably formulate if asked, might be something like, "The plural of 'brother' is 'brothers,' unless one wishes to sound antiquarian, poetic, biblical, or affected, in which case consider using 'brethren.'"

That is but one example among thousands that might be cited. The argument, then, is that the entire "system" of language is made up of such cases of usage that are created and modified over time by its users, who typically have no knowledge of or concern about the "system" itself. This is why language is an instance of "spontaneous order": "order" because it is relatively orderly, even if it changes over time; "spontaneous" because no single person intentionally created it.[7] Like baseball: No single person created the entire set of rules that currently characterize baseball. Not even the complete current *Handbook* exhausts the protocols and conventions of baseball, because there are far too many to capture in a single document, and in any case they are frequently changing.[8] Thus although many aspects of the complement of rules, protocols, and conventions of language (or baseball) can be traced, after the fact, to people who originated or modified them, no single person or group of persons deliberately designed the entire system. That is what Ferguson means when he says that these social orders are the results of human action but not of human design.

Two Further Facts about Language

Two other aspects of Smith's description of the rules affecting language are important to emphasize because they will loom large in Smith's later work: first, changes in language are a result of people's changing desires in their changing circumstances; second, though the rules are a human construction, they are neither arbitrary nor unenforced.

To the first, Smith writes that "the more enlarged experience" of the first language-users created a need for an expansion of their rudimentary language; he claims "their necessary occasions obliged them" to make the relevant changes (LRBL 203, §1). Thus their desire to "make their mutual wants intelligible to each other" (ibid.), combined with their changing circumstances, is what jointly led to the particular development of language that took place. It is important to see what this account of language's changes leaves out: There is no Important Person, or group of Important People, who foresee or foresaw what changes in language would best serve people's needs and thus announced the relevant changes. The changes arose instead organically from the bottom up, and for precisely this reason the changes are more closely tied to language users' needs than they would be if they had been the result of decrees by Important People. Now that does not mean that there are not grammar and linguistic experts, or that rules cannot be codified and taught to new users of the language. It means instead that such people are always doing rearguard action. Grammarians are not the source of the rules; at most they are maintainers of the rules. They act as a conservative force, a brake on innovation. Both innovation and brakes on innovation are important parts of a healthy, functioning language, just as they are of other large-scale human social institutions—a point that will take deep root in Smith. But the point here is simply a descriptive one about language: on Smith's account, changes normally percolate up from the bottom and are not decreed from the top down.

The second aspect is that the rules of language are, to borrow a phrase from David Hume, *artificial* but not *arbitrary*.[9] They are "artificial" in that they are constructed by humans. They do not occur naturally in the world, the way trees do, and they are not woven unalterably into the fabric of nature, as the laws of physics are. As Smith recounts in "Languages," word order is highly variable in the Latin tongue, but not in English. Similarly, oftentimes the meaning of a single word in one language requires several words in another language; Smith's example is the Latin word *arboris*, which translates into three words in English: "of the tree" (LRBL 211, §16). The fact that these differences among human languages exist show that the rules of language are not inherent in any external reality. Hence correct language usage is determined not by carefully studying, say, the objects being described, but rather by studying the way people use their words. Language is constructed by humans, who themselves vary in time, circumstance, and experience—and these variations are reflected in their languages.

Language rules are thus "artificial" because constructed by humans. But that does not mean they are arbitrary. For, first, there *are* rules of language. Language is not an anarchy with each person making things up for himself. Second, at any given time, most of the rules are commonly accepted; no debate is expected or even allowed. And third, infractions of the rules are usually noticed and frequently punished. Smith tells, for example, of the child learning to speak correctly: "A child that is just learning to speak, calls every person who comes to the house its papa or its mama" (LRBL 204, §1); and, "A child, speaking of itself, says, *Billy walks, Billy sits,* instead of *I walk, I sit*" (LRBL 219, §32). These are mistakes, Smith says, that soon get corrected—not by language police or the Board of Language Enforcement, but by the child's parents, the child's playmates, or other users of the language. If a child says, "I bringed my work home from school," the parent will, almost involuntarily, reply with "Brought!" before saying anything else. All new users of a language make mistakes, but the fact that they are recognized as mistakes and that people spontaneously correct the usages indicates that the rules are commonly accepted. Some contexts allow for wider latitude than others—think of poetry as opposed to college term-paper writing, for example—but there must always be rules, or, to repeat, the purpose of language, which Smith says is to allow effective communication, would be frustrated. One may not like the rules of one's language, or one might wish to change the pronunciation or usage of words or terms, but one had better exercise care in attempting to make unilateral changes: linguistic entrepreneurs, like economic entrepreneurs, probably fail many more times than they succeed, even if change and progress are the result primarily of such risk-takers.

Lessons from "Languages"

Smith's account of language development in this early essay adumbrates several central features of his later accounts of other major human social institutions, including morality and markets. Language is a system of order that arises spontaneously from the needs of its individual users and that changes over time in response to users' changing needs. Not only are the particular words and their usages spontaneously generated, but even rules about words and usage. Despite the variance of needs and circumstances at the individual level, there is enough continuity in experience among users of the language to respond to the need for stability and thus to develop commonly accepted and observed rules and conventions of usage. Moreover, these rules are enforced not from without but by the users themselves, and with punishments that vary depending on local judgments of the case at hand and its context.

The reader, furthermore, would be correct to detect in this essay the early hints of an argument that Smith will later develop into perhaps his most powerful, what we will call the Invisible Hand Argument: individuals, when seeking to satisfy their own localized desires will tend to behave in ways that will also benefit others—even others they do not know and about whom they therefore have no particular concern, and without their intending to do so.

Finally, one also sees in "Languages" an early example of Smith's desire to explain as much as he can with as few principles as possible, what I propose to call his Parsimony Principle (PP).[10] The PP informs nearly all of Smith's work. We see it in "Languages" when Smith argues that our desire to make our "mutual wants intelligible to each other" motivates the creation and development of language. We see it in TMS, when Smith relies on a single principle—that all people have a strong "desire for the mutual sympathy of sentiments"—to form a large part of Smith's explanation of human morality. We see it in *The Wealth of Nations* (WN) when Smith argues that several elements of a mature commercial economy are the result of our natural "propensity to truck, barter, and exchange one thing for another" (WN I.ii.1). We also see it in WN when Smith suggests that the desire to "better our condition"—a desire that "though generally calm and dispassionate, comes with us from the womb, and never leaves us till we go into the grave" (WN II.iii.28)—accounts for most of our economic behavior.

We see the PP moreover in another of Smith's essays, called "The History of Astronomy" (HA). HA was published 5 years after Smith's death, in a volume entitled *Essays on Philosophical Subjects*, brought out by Smith's friends and literary executors, Joseph Black and James Hutton. Though the essay was published posthumously, it was probably begun decades before Smith's death, perhaps as early as 1746, and was at one time intended to form a chapter of a much larger work, "giving," in the words of Black and Hutton, "a connected history of the liberal sciences and elegant arts" (EPS, 33).[11]

HA purports to explain what drives "philosophers"[12] to ask the questions they do and to seek explanations for the things they observe. As Smith explains in the essay, he thinks applying the PP is one of the hallmarks of a good philosopher, epitomized for Smith by Isaac Newton (1643–1727). Smith writes that "Philosophy is the science of the connecting principles of nature" (HA II.12), and Newton, as Smith explains, synthesized the disparate observations and principles of previous philosophers with only a few simple rules of motion and the principle of gravity.

> The superior genius and sagacity of Sir Isaac Newton, therefore, made the most happy, and, we may now say, the greatest and most admirable improvement that was ever made in philosophy, when he discovered, that he could join together the movements of the Planets by so familiar a principle of connection [namely, gravity], which completely removed all the difficulties the imagination had hitherto felt in attending to them. (HA IV.67)

There is a feeling of discomfort, Smith thought, in not being able to understand or explain what the hidden causes are that link together disparate events; by contrast, "the mind takes pleasure in observing the resemblances that are discoverable betwixt different objects" (HA I.10). This pleasure is heightened, Smith argued, as the number of disparate fields or observations or phenomena that a single principle can explain rises. Hence the glowing words Smith has for Newton: the fact that Newton's "gravity" could explain so much moved Smith to bestow upon it the elevated title of "greatest and most admirable improvement that was ever made in philosophy" (HA IV.67).

The PP thus forms an intellectual bridge that Smith, as well as others of the Scottish Enlightenment, saw linking both Newton and themselves to a new, improved, and distinctively modern scientific understanding of the world. In his 1687 *Principia*, in which he developed his theory of universal gravitation, Newton demonstrated the effects of "gravity" with astonishing success. But gravity would appear to be "action at a distance"—that is, one thing affecting another thing when they are not touching in any way—which many had thought to be impossible, or at least in need of an explanation. Newton's account seemed to some to be "occult," describing the effects of gravity without saying what, exactly, gravity itself is. It thus sounded to some as though he was not really describing the cause at all, only describing its effects.

Even if Newton could describe the motion of the planets, unless he explained what gravity itself is and how it works he leaves the impression that it works via some magical (hence "occult") powers. Newton's famous response to this charge, which appeared in the second edition of his *Principia*, was "hypotheses non fingo," or, "I make no hypotheses."[13] In other words, Newton was not interested to speculate about the intrinsic nature of "gravity" beyond describing what he could observe— and that was limited to its effects.

If some of Newton's contemporaries believed this was a fault of his work, Smith hailed it as one of its greatest virtues. Indeed, a posture of suspicion toward metaphysics and reliance instead on observed regularities would become one of the hallmark features that distinguishes many Scottish thinkers of this period, part of what gave rise to the methodology now called the Scottish Historical School. When approaching any problem of natural or moral philosophy, this School would counsel the inquirer not to begin with first philosophy or metaphysical principles, but rather first to investigate the relevant history. Look to past observations, past experiments, past data points, all in an effort to infer common patterns or regularities. If there is no, or little, historical evidence bearing on your topic, resort to "conjectural history," in the memorable phrase of Dugald Stewart: "when we cannot trace the process by which an event *has been* produced, it is often of importance to be able to show how it *may have been* produced by natural causes" (EPS, 292; emphasis in the original). Although this imaginative filling in of historical lacunae can also lead to speculation, the Scots of the eighteenth century were committed to avoiding, wherever possible, *a priori* deduction or metaphysical speculation.

The general preference for history and for principles inferred from empirical observation also informs most of Smith's work. The Parsimony Principle that so appealed to him referred to the ability of ingenious humans to discover or construct a rule or set of rules that would describe a large swath of observed phenomena. The lower the ratio of rules to phenomena, for Smith, the better. But the emphasis is on observing phenomena and on imagining a cause that links them. Thus he ends HA with the provocative claim that "we have been endeavouring to represent all philosophical systems as mere inventions of the imagination"; the "connecting principles" that the philosopher propounds are presented "as if they were the real chains which Nature makes use of to bind together her several operations" (HA IV.76). The implication is that we do not know whether they are in fact the chains Nature uses, only that they explain a range of phenomena. Perhaps, Smith suggests, this is the best that can be hoped for.

Smith's "History of Astronomy"

The full title of this essay is worth noting: "The Principles which Lead and Direct Philosophical Enquiries; Illustrated by the History of Astronomy." Because everything Smith wrote can plausibly be described as a philosophical inquiry, this is a good place to look if we wish to understand Smith's philosophical method. And that is indeed the chief value of this essay: It sets out what we might call Smith's philosophy of science, his understanding of what motivates the philosopher, what exactly it is the philosopher does, and how the philosopher ought to go about it. Contemporary scholar Gloria Vivenza has argued (2001: 28) that HA shows the methodological similarity of Smith's works, because even "scientific research" has its origins in sentiment— the psychological origin of scientific research, aiming to satisfy man's natural wonder and pacify his natural anxiety that lack of understanding can cause. But what does psychology have to do with astronomy?

Much of the first part of Smith's essay consists not of what one would perhaps expect from a "history of astronomy," but rather of a short disquisition on human psychology. Smith distinguishes three mental states—wonder, surprise, and admiration: "What is new and singular, excites that sentiment which, in strict propriety, is called Wonder; what is unexpected, Surprise; and what is great or beautiful, Admiration" (HA Intro.1). Why should we care about these mental states, or "sentiments" as Smith calls them? According to Smith, "the mind takes pleasure in observing the resemblances that are discoverable betwixt different objects" (HA II.1); moreover, when something new presents itself

> to us we are fond of referring "it" to some species or class of things, with all of which it has nearly exact resemblance; and though we often know no more about them than about it, yet we are apt to fancy that by being able to do so, we show

ourselves to be better acquainted with it, and to have a more thorough insight into its nature. (HA II.3)

As Smith makes clear, that is not yet science: it is merely looking for resemblances among things one observes, and categorizing experiences based on those resemblances.

When, however, we observe or experience something that bears no clear resemblance to what we already know, the "imagination and memory exert themselves to no purpose, and in vain look around all their classes of ideas in order to find one under which it may be arranged" (ibid.). This experience, Smith thinks, causes an anxiety—"wonder"—that is not altogether pleasant. It recurs with respect to anomalies we discover in previously held causal relations. If the "customary connection" between observed cause and effect "be interrupted, if one or more objects appear in an order quite different from that to which the imagination has been accustomed, and for which it is prepared," Smith believes we experience surprise and wonder (HA II.8); in this case, "the imagination feels a real difficulty," which can "soon fatigue it, and if repeated too often, disorder and disjoint its whole frame" (HA II.10). This, for Smith, is the birth of science, or at least of the inquiry that leads to science: the search for the "connecting principles of nature" that can unite and order the otherwise disjointed experiences (HA II.12). Smith writes:

> Philosophy, by representing the invisible chains which bind together all these disjointed objects, endeavours to introduce order into this chaos of jarring and discordant appearances, to allay this tumult of the imagination, and to restore it, when it surveys the great revolutions of the universe, to that tone of tranquillity and composure, which is both most agreeable in itself, and most suitable to its nature. Philosophy, therefore, may be regarded as one of those arts which address themselves to the imagination. (HA II.12)

The course of astronomical science, according to Smith's ensuing analysis, is constituted by successive discoveries of anxiety-producing anomalies and the attempt to imagine connecting principles that render the anomalies regular. It is in that sense that Smith can claim that science addresses itself to the imagination.

As Smith's analysis proceeds, it becomes clear that he presumes that the world is a coherent system, governed by laws that human inquiry can ascertain; indeed it is like a "machine" (HA IV.19; HAP 9), which thus enables scientific description. This is a Stoic, even Pythagorean, view of the world: orderly, rational, ultimately balanced and harmonious. For Vivenza, Smith's conclusions are "hypothetical and relativistic" (2001: 37): hypotheses framed to satisfy the imagination but always subject to future correction, and dependent on the psychology of the humans involved. Smith assumes that there is an external world, that that world is orderly, and that humans have the ability to learn about the world. On the other hand, he also seems to assume an epistemological skepticism: we can never be sure that the scientific model of the world we have is actually the correct one. We can know that it explains this or that set of data, we can know that its implications, if it is true, are thus and so; we can even know that no known observation contradicts it. And we can know that it satisfies the psychological anxiety that anomalies or unexplained events produce in us. All of that would give good reason to believe the hypothesis in question, whatever it is. But there always remains the possibility that future observations will be unlike past observations, or that enlarged experience will reveal new anomalies or unexplained events that our present hypothesis cannot account for. For this reason the good philosopher, Smith thought, offers his principles as tentative hypotheses, supported by experience, data, examples, or history but always open to correction on the basis of new evidence.

Is Smith a Scientific "Realist"?

Smith's philosophy of science thus constitutes a blend of what we might call "realist" and "anti-realist" strands: on the one hand, there is a (real) external world that operates on the basis of (real) causal principles; on the other, the philosophical theories we construct to describe this external world and its principles are "mere inventions of the imagination," and can be corroborated or disconfirmed but cannot be known to be true once and for all.[14]

Smith maintains this skeptical stance even in the case of the great Newton, whose principles Smith could scarcely imagine being proved false. Smith acknowledges that Newton's principles "have a degree of firmness and solidity that we should in vain look for in any other system" (HA IV.76). That is high

praise—but note that Smith does not say that Newton's principles are true, only that his principles have more "firmness and
solidity" than other systems. Smith continues that, given the
astonishing, even unprecedented, range of phenomena that
Newton's principles have been able to connect via his principle
of gravity, it should not surprise us that Newton's system

> should now be considered, not as an attempt to connect in the
> imagination the phaenomena of the Heavens, but as the great-
> est discovery that was ever made by man, the discovery of an
> immense chain of the most important and sublime truths, all
> closely connected together, by one capital fact [i.e., gravity],
> of the reality of which we have daily experience. (ibid.)

Thus Smith acknowledges that his reader will raise the success of
Newton's system—including its success at explaining anomalies
that undermined the systems of previous thinkers, like that of
Descartes—as an objection to Smith's hypothesis that scientific
theories are mere inventions of the imagination, imaginary
causal chains whose purpose is rather to assuage the anxiety that
anomaly-ridden theories are prone to raise than to describe correctly the actual causal chains in nature. If Newton's system is as
great as it clearly is, surely it is more than a mere invention of the
imagination, one might object. Smith anticipates the objection
and feels its power—and, it seems, senses the radical nature of
the position he is taking—yet he stands fast. It is not surprising,
he says, that Newton's system is *considered* to describe reality; yet
we still cannot know that it actually does.

Why not, exactly? What more does a scientific theory need in
order to pass beyond the realm of "mere invention of the imagination" to a description of actual reality? What seems required for us
to regard a scientific theory as no longer a theory but a fact is one
of two things: either we must have the ability to observe directly
the essence of things, not merely their qualities or effects; or we
must have observed the totality of facts in the world, past, present,
and future. Presumably God possesses both of these abilities;
humans, alas, possess neither. In articulating this position Smith
relies on an argument made by David Hume that we cannot
observe causation, only "constant conjunction."[15] Smith writes:

> When two objects, however unlike, have often been observed to
> follow each other, and have constantly presented themselves to

the senses in that order, they come to be so connected together in the fancy, that the idea of the one seems of its own accord, to call up and introduce that of the other. If the objects are still observed to succeed each other as before, this connection, or, as it has been called [by Hume], this association of their ideas, becomes stricter and stricter, and the habits of the imagination to pass from the conception of the one to that of the other, grows more and more rivetted and confirmed. (HA II.7)

This "rivetted" association of ideas is what Smith (and Hume) takes to be "cause" and "effect." Note, then, wherein a causal relation consists: in an "association of ideas," not an association of the things themselves. Thus Smith, following Hume, argues that our knowledge of causality is limited by what we can observe—and that is a succession, even a constant conjunction, of events, but not "causality" itself. We infer that there exists a causal relation between two constantly conjoined events, but that is an inference that, strictly speaking, goes beyond the observations. Smith's argument is that the imputation of a causal relation, which would connect two events necessarily rather than merely contingently, is (a) prompted by our psychological desire to alleviate the anxiety we otherwise would feel if there were no connecting principle between the events and (b) exists in our imagination.

Smith's position would seem to reduce science to an exercise in human psychology instead of the standard view that it is an attempt to understand the nature of an external reality. It would not, however, entail the extreme view that we can know nothing at all about the external world, an objection sometimes pressed. What rescues Smith from this highly dubious consequence of his position is that he does not deny that our observations of the world can be genuine and accurate. Smith believes there really is an external world and our observations can lead us to true beliefs about it. His claim is only that our potentially true beliefs about the external world are dependent on, and thus limited by, our actual observations. If we have not observed something, we cannot know whether what we believe about it is true or not. Since we have not observed "causality," we cannot know exactly what it is; since we have not observed "gravity," we cannot know exactly what it is. We have observed the *effects* of both, however, and hence we can measure, compare, and discover patterns in their effects, even if the things themselves remain behind a veil.

Smith's is an unconventional interpretation of the origins and development of science, to say the least, and it raises at least as many questions as it does answers. Can a scientific theory on Smith's account ever be regarded as *true*? Indeed, what would it even mean for it to be true, on that account? Is science really only an epistemological endeavor, discovering the limits of our own knowledge, and not an ontological one, discovering the nature of things in themselves? Would Smith's account leave science without any ultimate foundations, without any grounding in an independently existing external world? I leave these questions to the reader, as well as the question of whether the awkward implications of Smith's philosophy of science in fact constitute a *reductio ad absurdum* refutation of it.[16]

What I would emphasize, however, is that the method outlined in this essay again demonstrates Smith's privileging empirical observation as a source, perhaps *the* source, of human knowledge as well as the proper object of scientific or philosophical inquiries. It shows moreover that Smith is not only unconcerned with the absence of a metaphysical grounding of scientific theory, but he seems positively suspicious of such groundings. Hume had argued famously that if one comes upon a volume in the library that does not contain mathematical demonstrations or actual or conjectural histories—if it contains, in other words, metaphysical speculations, scholastic disquisitions, or sophistical rhetorical flourishes—"commit it then to the flames."[17] What we can expect to characterize Smith's investigations, then, is a reliance on actual, real-world examples, on observations, and on experiences; we should expect him to introduce principles that unite as many disparate phenomena as possible but that are hypothetical and always subject to revision or rejection based on future observation. We will find these features in all Smith's investigations.

Self-interest

Before leaving the discussion of HA, I wish to register one more aspect of Smith's argument that will bear on an issue we explore later. In HA, Smith considers the possibility that what drives scientists is an expectation of gain rather than a desire for knowledge. Smith's response:

[Scientists'] imagination, which accompanies with ease and delight the regular progress of nature, is stopped and embarrassed by those seeming incoherences; they excite their wonder, and seem to require some chain of intermediate events, which, by connecting them with something that has gone before, may thus render the whole course of the universe consistent and of a piece. Wonder, therefore, and not any expectation of advantage from its discoveries, is the first principle which prompts mankind to the study of Philosophy, of that science which pretends to lay open the concealed connections that unite the various appearances of nature; and they pursue this study for its own sake, as an original pleasure or good in itself, without regarding its tendency to procure them the means of many other pleasures. (HA III.3)

When writing this passage Smith may have had in mind Aristotle's story[18] of the ancient Greek philosopher Thales, who eventually tired of the mocking he endured for being an absent-minded philosopher. So he studied the weather patterns and was able to determine that conditions were favorable for a bumper crop of olives next season. Based on his prediction, he bought all the olive presses, which people were happy to sell him at a low price since it was the off-season; when the bumper crop came, as Thales predicted, he was able to sell the presses back to the farmers at a princely profit. Thales apparently gave the money away, but he proved his point that a philosopher could make money if he wanted to: he simply chooses to focus his attentions elsewhere. Philosophical or scientific researches had, already in Smith's day, led to technological innovations that could turn a profit, and many other inventions could lead to increased productivity that might enable greater leisure. In this passage Smith argues that these motivations are secondary at best. What motivates the philosopher or scientist is "an original pleasure or good in itself, without regarding its tendency to procure [. . .] the means of many other pleasures" (HA III.3).

What this means is that according to Smith human beings—at least some of them—are sometimes motivated by something other than crass materialism or crude self-interest. One of the enduring criticisms of the capitalistic economic system of which Smith is often regarded as the patron saint is that it appeals only to our self-interest, or perhaps assumes that the only motivating factor in human behavior is self-interest. Smith here takes a different position. We shall later examine Smith's view of natural human motivation, but for now we can say that in this essay Smith acknowledges that philosophical progress is motivated not by an expectation of advantages to be gained but rather for the sake of the study itself.

Notes

[1] See Berry (1997), Broadie (2001), and Haakonssen (1981).

[2] Available here: http://mlb.mlb.com/mlb/official_info/official_ rules/foreword.jsp.

[3] A summary is available here: http://mlb.mlb.com/mlb/official_ info/umpires/strike_zone.jsp.

[4] Since Thomas Kuhn (1996 [1962]) there has been considerable discussion about the extent to which science is in fact a progressive, cumulative enterprise. One consequence of this discussion has been the proposal that scientific theories actually say more about us—about our desires, our psychological makeup, and so on—than they do about the external reality they purport to describe. It turns out that Smith was alive to this possibility, a point to which we shall return shortly.

[5] Ferguson (1995 [1767]) III.2, p. 119.

[6] Smith uses "brethren" 20 times in TMS and "brothers" 14 times.

[7] For detailed discussion of spontaneous-order explanations and their relation to and use in Smith, see Craig Smith (2006).

[8] Consider, for example, the perhaps superstitious convention of never stepping on the foul line when taking the field: most major league baseball players observe this convention, though it is not part of any rulebook.

[9] Hume wrote, "Tho' the rules of justice be *artificial*, they are not *arbitrary*. Nor is the expression improper to call them *laws of nature*, if by *natural* we understand what is common to any species, or even if we confine it to mean what is inseparable from the species" (*Treatise of Human Nature* 3.2.1.19; emphasis in the original).

[10] Smith's PP is similar but not identical to what is known as Ockham's Razor, usually rendered as "do not needlessly multiply entities." Smith's PP, which attempts to explain as much as possible with as few principles as possible, might thus be the positive corollary—that is, telling the researcher what to do—to the negative Ockham's Razor, which tells the researcher what not to do.

[11] The reader interested in exploring the reasons for believing the essay to have been composed in the mid- to late-1740s might

consult the editor's introduction to EPS, 5–11 or Ross (1995), chapter 7.

[12] Smith used the term "philosopher" in its eighteenth-century sense of investigator into the nature of things. There were two kinds of philosophers, natural and moral: the natural philosopher, like Newton, inquired into the nature of the physical world in which humans find themselves, which today would include the natural sciences; the moral philosopher, like Smith, inquired into all things relating to human nature and human action, which today would include most disciplines in humanities and in social sciences.

[13] Scholium Generale, rev. 2nd ed., *Philosophiae Naturalis Principia Mathematica* (1713 [1687]).

[14] Here Smith might differ from Kuhn, if Kuhn is interpreted to mean that all aspects of science and scientific knowledge are dependent on conceptual "paradigms," an interpretation that Kuhn himself later in his life repudiated (see Kuhn [1977]). In relying, as I argue, on a notion of disconfirmation but not confirmation, Smith may have anticipated Popper's theory of the progress of science. See Popper (2000 [1963]). For more on the relation of Smith to Newton, see Montes (2004), chapter 5.

[15] See Hume (2000 [1739–40]) 1.3.12 and passim.

[16] For discussion of some of these issues, see Schliesser (2005).

[17] Hume (1975 [1748]), 165.

[18] In his *Politics* 1259a9–18.

Chapter 3

Smith's Genealogy of Morality

In 1759, Smith stitched together the lecture notes he had been developing and using since he took up the position of Professor of Moral Philosophy at the University of Glasgow in 1752. The result was Smith's first book, *The Theory of Moral Sentiments* (TMS). The book bears many of the marks we would expect from its origin as lecture notes. Smith's students would have been young men, many teenagers, the former fact revealed in a handful of remarks that remained in the book form in which Smith speaks of "our" sex as opposed to the other, "fair" sex. It is also repetitive in parts, presumably reflecting the need to remind students of what went on earlier in the course; it employs many examples to make its points, when one might have sufficed; it includes several digressions and even, on occasion, attempts at humor; and it contains regular exhortations to virtue and even to proper religion, as would have been expected and appropriate for the chair of moral philosophy in his instruction of university students.

Yet for all this TMS represents an astounding philosophical achievement: it marks a nearly revolutionary break from ancient and modern moral philosophy, and it builds on the insights of other philosophers—Hume in particular—to inaugurate a new and distinctive school of moral thought. Smith introduces in this work a new standard of moral judgment, the "impartial spectator," which is an improvement on similar notions others had employed; he introduces a single motivational principle, the "desire for mutual sympathy of sentiments" (MSS), which animates most human moral phenomena; he explains and accounts for both moral agreement and disagreement; he raises a question few had asked before, namely how people transition from amoral infants to moralized adults; and he provides his own novel explanation for this transition, an explanation that subsequent research has shown to be surprisingly accurate.

TMS as a Book

TMS went through six editions during Smith's lifetime. The second and sixth editions received the largest revisions. Part VI, "Of the Character of Virtue," was an entirely new addition in the sixth and final edition of TMS, which appeared a few weeks before Smith died in 1790. Thus the first edition appeared when Smith was 36 years old, and edition six when he was 67; if we count the years he had been delivering the lectures on which TMS was based, that means that he worked on the materials in TMS with some regularity for nearly 40 years. It is not surprising that there should be differences between the early and the later editions; indeed, it would be astonishing if there were none. An old quip has it that if a scholar does not change his mind every 10 years, he is not thinking hard enough. And accordingly Smith did indeed change his mind about some things. I think that the central parts of TMS's argument did not change, however, and hence in what follows I shall focus on those aspects that remain constant, and I shall regard the sixth and final edition as the definitive one.[1]

TMS has seven parts. Most of the central philosophical elements of Smith's explanation of human morality are contained in the first three parts: his notions of "propriety" and "merit," his explanation of one's conscience and the standard of the "impartial spectator," and their dependence on a natural desire for MSS. Part four is a discussion of the connection between our moral sentiments and utility, largely in response to Hume's argument. Part five discusses the extent to which our moral sentiments are dependent on "custom and fashion," and are thus variable or relative. Part six is a sketch of what Smith believes the virtuous life looks like; this part contains some of the most provocative statements of TMS, which have added interest because they are the product of Smith's most mature reflection. Finally, part seven is a history of ethical theory: Smith discusses the main elements of several important other moral theories and explores the extent to which they do or do not agree with his own.

TMS is a rich and complex book, filled with striking analyses and claims. We cannot address them all here. So I propose the following: I shall first give an overview of what I believe Smith's theory is meant to show; then I shall give brief elaborations of several of the main elements of the theory.

Getting the Theory off the Ground: the Desire for MSS

Smith believes that common moral standards arise on the basis of an interactive process that takes place in and over specific historical locations. Since human beings live in different times and places, the systems of commonly shared moral standards vary in their details; but since human beings also share, in some specific relevant respects, a common human nature, their moral systems also enjoy significant overlap. The element of human nature most crucial for Smith's account is what he calls the *desire for MSS*. According to Smith's usage, "sympathy" is broader than mere pity or feeling sorry for someone:

> Pity and compassion are words appropriated to signify our fellow-feeling with the sorrow of others. Sympathy, though its meaning was, perhaps, originally the same, may now, however, without much impropriety, be made use of to denote our fellow-feeling with any passion whatever. (TMS I.i.i.5)

Thus the desire for the MSS is, for Smith, the desire to see our own sentiments, whatever they are, reflected in others: "nothing pleases us more than to observe in other men a fellow-feeling with all the emotions of our own breast; nor are we ever so much shocked as by the appearance of the contrary" (TMS I.i.2.1).

This desire is the *sine qua non* of Smith's theory. Its ubiquitous presence in human beings is what drives us into society, what motivates much of our conversation and conduct, what leads us to moderate our sentiments and behavior so that they more closely accord with what others would expect, and what ultimately gives rise to the habits and rules of moral judgment that come to constitute what we can call the "system" of commonly shared morality. Moreover, without this universal desire, the rest of Smith's theory of moral sentiments would not get off the ground. Although there are other desires Smith says all humans have,[2] Smith thus rests an enormous part of the burden of his explanation of moral systems on the workings out of this single principle. Given Smith's Parsimony Principle, it is not surprising that he would seek to explain a large range of phenomena with one principle. Smith takes the desire for MSS to be an invisible, imaginary chain that he has discovered that, like Newton's gravity, can explain a surprisingly large range of human moral life. But can this one principle shoulder that burden?

The Genealogy of Morality

Smith's TMS is largely an exercise in what we might today call "moral psychology." It seeks to understand what moral judgments people make, why they make them, how they make them, and what the mechanisms are that explain why nearly all people develop moral codes and why people's moral codes significantly overlap with the codes of their loved ones and friends. This kind of discussion of human morality approaches the topic as a modern-day anthropologist, historian, psychologist, or cognitive scientist might, or even the way a primatologist might approach a central aspect of the social behavior of chimpanzees.[3] That is not to say that Smith thought there was no difference between humans and other animals; rather, it means that he proposed to treat human morality like any other complex, large-scale, observable phenomenon and to examine its nature and its effects.

Here are some facts that struck Smith and animated his investigation. First, nearly all human beings transition during their lifetimes from having no moral code as infants and small children to having complex, sophisticated moral codes as adults. Second, all known human communities have prevailing moral codes. Third, the moral codes of these communities overlap but are not identical. And fourth, some aspects of moral codes change over time yet other aspects seem to endure. What Smith wanted to know is what could account for these facts, and he wanted to address them as a moral philosopher or scientist, following lead of Newton: Study the phenomena, look for regularities, propose mechanisms that can explain the regularities, test the putative mechanisms against future or larger data. It is in this way that Smith's theory is, as I call it, a "genealogy of morality": It seeks to explain and describe morality, to determine its origins and its nature. Criticizing it, as well as encouraging others to abide by the proper moral code, is of secondary concern to Smith. That does not mean he is unconcerned with the task of being a "moralist," as we might call it, as against the task of being a "scientist." We find Smith wearing both these hats in TMS. It means instead that he is concerned first and foremost with the scientific aspects.

Let us begin with this question: How does Smith propose that individuals develop moral codes? We are born, Smith thinks, with no morality whatsoever. A baby knows only its own wants, with no notion of a proper (or improper) thing to ask for, of a proper (or improper) way to ask for it, or, for that matter, of shame or remorse for having asked for something it should not have asked for. Hence the baby attempts to have its wants satisfied simply by alarming its caregiver with howls and cries. The baby is not to blame, however, in these outrageous self-indulgences: not only is it not yet capable of considering such matters as *propriety* or *others' interests*, but it is probably also encouraged in its selfishness, says Smith, by its overly indulgent parent or nurse.[4]

According to Smith it is not until the baby has grown to a child and begins playing with its mates that the child has the jolting experience of realizing that he is not the center of everyone's life, only of his own. Smith writes that this is the child's introduction into the "great school of self-command" (TMS III.3.22): it is on being with others and having the experience of being *judged* by them—even if it is only implicitly, by, say, not playing with him or ignoring his demands—that the child has the distinct displeasure associated with not sharing a MSS. And displeasure it is. Taking a small but telling example, Smith writes,

> A man is mortified when, after having endeavoured to divert the company, he looks round and sees that nobody laughs at his jests but himself. On the contrary, the mirth of the company is highly agreeable to him, and he regards this correspondence of their sentiments with his own as the greatest applause. (TMS I.i.2.1)

When one becomes aware that others do not share one's sentiments—that is, that no "correspondence," "harmony," "concord," or "sympathy" of sentiments obtains—one feels embarrassed, chagrined, awkward, isolated. The exact degree of one's feeling of isolation depends on the particulars of the situation, but it is never pleasant. Returning to the case of the child spurned by his schoolmates, after the initial jolt, Smith believes the child begins to cast about to find a way to relieve the displeasure. Eventually the child learns to modify his behavior to more closely match that of his playmates. When he does so, *voilà*: an exquisite new pleasure is experienced, that of the MSS, and a new and permanent desire for that pleasure has been aroused. From that point on, according to Smith, the child regularly engages in trial-and-error investigation into what behaviors will achieve this sympathy and thus satisfy this desire.

This investigation encourages the individual to discover and then adopt rules of behavior and judgment that increase the chance of achieving mutual sympathy. By the time the child has become an adult, he has adopted a wide range of principles of behavior and judgment that he applies in many different situations. Everyone else, moreover, is engaging in precisely the same investigation:

> As the person who is principally interested in any event is pleased with our sympathy, and hurt by the want of it, so we, too, seem to be pleased when we are able to sympathize with him, and to be hurt when we are unable to do so. We run not only to congratulate the successful, but to condole with the afflicted; and the pleasure which we find in the conversation of one whom in all the passions of his heart we can entirely sympathize with, seems to do more than compensate the painfulness of that sorrow with which the view of his situation affects us. On the contrary, it is always disagreeable to feel that we cannot sympathize with him, and instead of being pleased with this exemption from sympathetic pain, it hurts us to find that we cannot share his uneasiness. (TMS I.i.2.6)

Our strong desire for mutual sympathy of all our sentiments leads to reciprocity and mutual seeking of sympathy, thereby creating an invisible-hand mechanism that Smith thinks generates commonly shared standards of behavior and judgment, indeed a commonly shared *system* of morality. It is an *invisible* hand because the agents in question do not intend to create a shared system of morality—they intend only to achieve mutual

sympathy here, now, with this person. In so doing, however, they
(unintentionally) create the behavioral habits, precedents, and
protocols that will generate and maintain a shared system of
expectations and sentiments, with their correlated judgments,
reproaches, and praises.

A Marketplace of Morality

The mechanism at work here is similar to those at work in other
arenas of human social life. Consider economic markets. On
Smith's view, an economic market exists wherever people
exchange goods or services in an effort to improve their condition.[5] A newcomer to a market might initially have no idea what
his goods or services will command, so he tries various exchange
methods, rates, and partners, until he hits upon some combination that succeeds. And then he too feels a pleasure—of his
condition being bettered, which Smith claims in *The Wealth of
Nations* (WN) is our constant, abiding motivation.[6] There are
in fact several similarities between Smith's conception of an
economic marketplace and what one might call the Smithian
"moral marketplace." First, in both cases, the persons principally
concerned initially had little to go on: they just had to try
something out. Second, in both cases the persons principally
concerned might have been abashed and felt displeasure at
having been initially spurned, which is the likely outcome of
one's first sallies in either market. Third, just as a person in an
economic market can afterwards regret the exchange he made,
so too a person can achieve a mutual sympathy with someone,
only later to regret, even be ashamed at, having done so with this
person, or to this degree, or regarding this object. Fourth,
efficient or useful rules of behavior arise as a consequence of
people enjoying the liberty to experiment with exchanging, or
attempting to exchange, as they judge fit. If they are restricted in
advance as to what, how, or with whom they may exchange, they
may not discover the most useful patterns.

> The great pleasure of conversation and society, besides, arises
> from a certain correspondence of sentiments and opinions, from
> a certain harmony of minds, which like so many musical instru-
> ments coincide and keep time with one another. But this most

delightful harmony cannot be obtained unless there is a free communication of sentiments and opinions. (TMS VII.iv.28)

Finally, the process of trial-and-error discovery is supplemented crucially in both cases by *negotiation*: the person principally concerned (PPC) tries to convince potential mutual sympathizers or exchange partners that the behaviors or judgments, or the goods or services, *should* be sympathized with or exchanged for. He offers reasons or arguments, he exhorts, he demands, he pleas, he cajoles, he begs, he harangues. You and I try to talk each other into sympathizing with one another's sentiments,[7] just as you and I might try to talk each other into selling one of our proffered goods at the other's proffered price. These negotiations take many different forms, they range over an indefinitely wide variety of issues, and they frequently end in failure. Even in failure, however, they are instructive; and when they are successful, they can establish precedents that both we later on and others can imitate. The precedents become habits, then rules and principles; they can then come to constitute a system of rules or principles.

Thus Smith's account of the genesis both of shared *moral* standards, which include commonly held conceptions of propriety and merit, is structurally similar to his account of shared *economic* standards, which include commonly accepted prices, conditions of exchange, contracts, and so on. Both systems are turbulent at the micro-level and subject to change over time, but both also settle on, or work toward, a modified equilibrium at the macro-level: the individual decisions that make up the systems are, on the individual level, often unpredictable and variegated; yet they (unintentionally) give rise to a larger system that is relatively coherent and susceptible of general description.[8]

Central Elements

Because of the similarities between Smith's understanding of both moral and economic systems, I call his account a "market model," and the process giving rise to the systems a "market mechanism." I discuss the economic model in Chapters 6 and 7. Here, let us turn to elaborations of several of the central elements of Smith's moral theory.

Propriety and Merit. Smith divides the moral judgment into two complementary parts, each of which can operate independently:

> The sentiment or affection of the heart from which any action proceeds, and upon which its whole virtue or vice must ultimately depend, may be considered under two different aspects, or in two different relations; first, in relation to the cause which excites it, or the motive which gives occasion to it; and secondly, in relation to the end which it proposes, or the effect which it tends to produce. (TMS I.i.3.5)

The former Smith calls "propriety" (and its contrary "impropriety"), the latter he calls "merit" (and its contrary "demerit"). When we pass a moral judgment on a person's actions, we will have one or the other of two aspects of the actions in mind: whether the person's actions were caused by sentiments that were fitting responses to the situation in which the person found himself, and whether the consequences of the actions were beneficial to others. An action prompted by sentiments that are fitting given the circumstances is "proper"; an action whose consequences benefit, or tend to benefit, those affected by it is "meritorious."

How do we know whether the action we are judging is proper or meritorious? Smith thinks we engage in an imaginative switching-of-places with the PPC; we imagine ourselves in his position, we imagine what our own reaction would have been to the circumstances he faces, and then we compare our imagined reaction to his actual reaction. If there is a "concord" or "harmony" between the two—if our imagined sentiments harmonize, or sympathize, with those of the PPC—then we approve of the person's sentiments and thus his conduct as being "proper"; if not, then we judge them to be "improper."

> When we judge in this manner of any affection, as proportioned or disproportioned to the cause which excites it, it is scarce possible that we should make use of any other rule or canon but the correspondent affection in ourselves. If, upon bringing the case home to our breast, we find that the sentiments which it gives occasion to, coincide and tally with our own, we necessarily approve of them as proportioned and

suitable to their objects; if otherwise, we necessarily disapprove of them, as extravagant and out of proportion. (TMS I.1.3.9)

Thus our moral judgments are, on Smith's account, relative to and dependent upon our own experiences. That may make it sound as if our moral judgments enjoy no objectivity, but they in fact enjoy an *intersubjective objectivity*. Because each person takes pleasure from MSS (and a displeasure from an antipathy), each of us has a natural incentive to cultivate sentiments that more nearly approximate those of others. We feel our own sentiments quite strongly, but we know from experience that others often would not imaginatively sympathize with strong sentiments; thus we "always endeavour to bring down our passion to that pitch, which the particular company we are in may be expected to go along with" (TMS i.i.3.9). As everyone else is doing the same, the result is a mutual gravitation toward a kind of general consensus about what kinds of sentiments are appropriate in what circumstances. People's sentiments may not perfectly coincide, but the incentives to move in mutually agreeable directions typically make enough headway to allow for settled consensuses to arise. "Though they will never be unisons," Smith says of the agent's and his observers' respective sentiments, "they may be concords, and this is all that is wanted or required" (TMS I.i.4.7).

To illustrate, consider joke-telling, a favorite example of Smith's.[9] A moment's reflection reveals that there are rules determining what kind of jokes one may tell in what company, how long one may laugh at a joke, and whether one should consider a given joke funny. A bit more reflection reveals just how nuanced and context-dependent these rules are: they may depend on the age, sex, religion, or ethnicity of one's audience, how well one knows the members of one's audience, what the setting is, perhaps by what time of day it is, and so on. Who develops these rules? Who enforces them? The answer to both is: *we* do—though usually unconsciously. Like the rules of language, the rules of joke-telling are a product of unintentional order, habits based on experience. We enforce them by condemning—in various and sometimes exquisitely subtle ways—infractions of them, and we reinforce them by observing them. There may be play in the rules, cases in which a range of kinds of jokes might be appropriate, but typically there are also examples that people would

consider clearly beyond the pale. Thus there would be "proper"
and "improper" jokes, "proper" and "improper" laughing at
jokes, and so on, and the process for determining propriety in
the case of joke-telling is the same as it is in the passing of judgments on other sentiments. One imagines oneself in the other's
place, imagines what sentiments one would likely have experienced, compares the two, and thence renders the judgment.
Similarly with determining whether a person's anger is proper or
not, whether a person's happiness or sadness is proper or not,
and so on through all the other passions and sentiments.[10]

By comparison with "propriety," the complementary part
of the moral judgment, "merit," is relatively straightforward.
A judgment about merit or demerit, according to Smith, depends
"upon the beneficial or hurtful effects which the affection
proposes or tends to produce, depends the merit or demerit,
the good or ill desert of the action to which it gives occasion"
(TMS II.intro.2). So for Smith a complete moral judgment comprises *both* a "principled" part—whether the relevant sentiments
comport with the relevant rules or not—*and* a "consequential-
ist" part—whether the effects of the action(s) prompted by the
sentiments are beneficial or not.

A perhaps unexpected twist in Smith's account, however, is
that he thinks we judge whether the sentiments prompting a
person's actions are meritorious by determining whether their
intended object—the person who is intended to be benefitted
(or harmed) by the action—experiences justified gratitude or
resentment. If that person experiences gratitude that is justified,
it prompts the observer to reward the agent; if the person
experiences resentment that is justified, it prompts the observer
to punish the agent. How does one determine whether the
object's gratitude or resentment is justified? By again comparing
that person's sentiments to what would be one's own sentiments
as one imagines oneself in that person's position. Thus Smith's
argument that the rendering of moral judgments is effected
by imaginatively switching places with the people involved
explains the central aspect of both parts of the complete moral
judgment. In both cases, one's imagination is required, and it
must do quite a bit of work: it must take into account all the
relevant details of the PPC, of the situation in question, and of
the object of the PPC's intentions; then it must imagine what
one's own sentiments would be, in light of all those details, if

one were in the PPC's position; and then it must do all of the same for the person who, as Smith puts it, is "acted upon."

Additionally, Smith thinks we must determine whether we think that the agent's motives were justified or not in acting toward the object the way the agent did:

> Our heart must adopt the principles of the agent, and go along with all the affections which influenced his conduct, before it can entirely sympathize with, and beat time to, the gratitude of the person who has been benefitted by his actions. (TMS II.i.4.1)

This means that on Smith's analysis merit is a "compounded sentiment," made up partly of our relative sympathy with the sentiments of the agent and partly of our relative sympathy with the sentiments of the person acted upon. Thus there are four possibilities: (1) sympathy with both the agent and the object; (2) sympathy with the agent but antipathy with the object; (3) antipathy with the agent but sympathy with the object; and (4) antipathy for both. Smith gives examples of some but not all of the cases. For example, reading about Borgia or Nero, he says, gives us an antipathy for their sentiments and a sympathy with the sentiments of those whom they "insulted, murdered, or betrayed" (TMS Ii.i.5.6). I leave it to the reader to imagine examples of the other cases. Suffice it to say that Smith's picture of human psychology grows complex here, though that does not, perhaps, mean it is inaccurate. Imagine, for example, observing one's parents fighting: In such a case one might well have a divided sympathy, for exactly the reasons Smith describes.

To summarize. Smith's analysis proposes that when we judge a person's actions, we judge it in two aspects: "first, in relation to the cause or object which excites" the sentiments that led to the person's actions; "secondly, in relation to the end which it proposes, or to the effect which it tends to produce" (TMS II. intro.2). The first he calls the actions' "propriety," the second he calls its "merit." A *proper* action deserves *approbation*, and a *meritorious* action deserves *reward*; an *improper* action deserves *disapprobation* and a *demeritorious* action deserves *punishment*. Moreover, the person toward whom a meritorious action is directed will, or should, feel a justified *gratitude*, as the person toward whom a demeritorious action is directed will, or should, feel a justified *resentment.*[11] That is Smith's outline of the complete moral judgment. It is based on people's sentiments, and the standards one uses to determine propriety and merit are developed and honed by experience of people's (including one's own) past judgments in similar circumstances. Finally, the rendering of the judgment itself is based on an imaginary comparison one makes between the sentiments and actions of the person one is judging and what one's own sentiments and actions would be if one were in that person's place.

MSS and Negotiation. It turns out, Smith believes, that the level of propriety of most sentiments lies "in a certain mediocrity," by which he means that the "pitch" of one's passions must not be too high or too low (TMS I.ii.intro.1). This is the natural, and expected, result of the negotiation Smith believes goes on between the person feeling the sentiment, who wants others to enter into his sentiment, and the spectators, who are not as inclined to enter into them: they settle on a level somewhere in the middle. As these negotiations are executed over and over again, patterns emerge that become, as it were, the default settings. Level L_1 of passion P_1 is typically deemed appropriate in situation S_1; level L_2 of passion P_2 is deemed appropriate in situation S_2; and so on. Keeping close to those levels will typically result in a MSS, while straying too far from them will result in a lack of sympathy or even an antipathy unless there are special circumstances in play.

Smith argues that the "mediocrity" that constitutes propriety "is different in different passions" and "is high in some, and low in others" (TMS I.ii.intro.2). He spends time in part one of TMS giving some indication of where he thinks the levels fall for various passions, as well as discussing some of the factors that influence those levels of propriety. Later, in part six, Smith will give a more complete picture of what he believes constitutes virtue for people in different walks of life. I shall not rehearse Smith's results here, but it is important to note what exactly Smith believes he is exploring. He is simply laying out the contours of what people actually judge to be proper or improper, meritorious or demeritorious. He is not endorsing those views, he is not attempting to encourage people to act morally, and he is not trying to derive moral judgments from on high. Smith's is an empirical, grounded investigation into the phenomenon of human judgment-making. Smith is a scientist or philosopher, not a moral preacher.[12] Smith would therefore want his analysis to be judged on its empirical accuracy—whether it does in fact comport with observations about human judgment-making—and not on whether the judgments or standards it discusses are good ones, whether they should be endorsed or criticized, and so on. Indeed, when discussing the perhaps controversial topic of justified resentment, Smith writes:

> Let it be considered too, that the present inquiry is not concerning a matter of right, if I may say so, but concerning a matter of fact. We are not at present examining upon what principles a perfect being would approve of the punishment of bad actions; but upon what principles so weak and imperfect a creature as man actually and in fact approves of it. (TMS II.i.5.10)

If one were to worry that Smith's description of moral judgments leaves them unacceptably untethered to a permanent, transcendent, unchanging, or supernatural foundation, the worry might be justified but not relevant to Smith's analysis. Similarly, a person might worry, for example, that a claim that human beings evolved from earlier, nonhuman progenitors might diminish the respect people have for human life. That worry might be justified, but it would not affect the truth or falsity of the claim in question. Smith's analysis aims to describe the facts of human morality; his examination might be factually right or wrong, but it could not be morally good or bad.

As mentioned, the search for MSS in which all people engage, according to Smith, often comprehends an element of negotiation. Each of us wants the pleasure associated with mutual sympathy, so each of us tries to get others to sympathize with his own sentiments. One aspect of this negotiation that has not been mentioned is Smith's suggestion that it develops certain skills in us. The desire to achieve MSS leads us to develop powers of persuasion, as well as the ability to describe our situation in vivid detail, all in an effort to increase the chances that others will sympathize with our sentiments. It also leads us to develop our power of imagination: sometimes achieving a MSS requires us to fill out in our imagination many details and to run a complex virtual reality movie, as it were, keeping track of these details and how they will or might interact. The better able we are to do this, the more accurate—meaning the more likely to lead to MSS—our imagination, and thus our judgment, can become. According to Smith, to judge accurately, one

> must, first of all, endeavour, as much as he can, to put himself in the situation of the other, and to bring home to himself *every little circumstance* of distress which can possibly occur to the sufferer. He must adopt the whole case of his companion *with all its minutest incidents*; and strive to render as perfect as possible, that imaginary change of situation upon which his sympathy is founded. (TMS I.i.4.6; emphasis supplied)

That is a lot to keep in mind. When we fail to achieve a MSS, Smith says it is usually due to one of two circumstances. The failure

> arises either from the different degrees of attention, which our different habits of life allow us to give easily to the several parts of those complex objects, or from the different degrees of natural acuteness in the faculty of the mind to which they are addressed. (TMS I.i.4.2)

As one might expect, some will become better at wielding this complex skill of imagining and judgment-making than others.

Although this part of Smith's analysis would not qualify, perhaps, as a proper moral injunction, it does indicate that there are some incentives at work leading us in a mutually beneficial way. Given that you desire MSS, and given that your chances of achieving it increase with the delicacy of your imagination and the accuracy of your judgments, you should strive to hone your skills of imagining others' situations. You will thereby increase the chances of satisfying your own desire of MSS, while simultaneously—if unintentionally—providing others with something they desire as well, namely MSS. Though Smith does not use the phrase "invisible hand" here,[13] I suggest that this is an invisible-hand argument nonetheless. Borrowing language from Smith's WN, which applies here perfectly: As each of us strives to satisfy his own desire for MSS, each of us is led to behave in ways that enable others to satisfy their desires for MSS, thereby encouraging behavior that "is most advantageous to the society" (WN IV.ii.4); thus each of us "is in this, as in many other cases, led by an invisible hand to promote an end that was no part of his intention" (WN IV.ii.9).

The Impartial Spectator. Propriety and merit are the bases of the moral judgments we pass on others' sentiments and actions, according to Smith. What about judgments we pass on ourselves? Another aspect of human judgment-making is *self*-judgments: we often approve or disapprove of our own sentiments or actions, we often in retrospect feel pride or shame for what we felt or did, and we often make resolutions to behave in certain ways or to refrain from behaving in certain ways in the future. Smith accounts for this aspect of human morality by reference to the perspective of what he calls the "impartial spectator."

Smith argues that the process of passing judgment on oneself is, despite what one might initially suspect, quite similar to that of passing judgment on others. In the latter case, as we have seen, "We either approve or disapprove of the conduct of another man according as we feel that, when we bring his case home to ourselves, we either can or cannot entirely sympathize with the sentiments and motives which directed it"; similarly,

> we either approve or disapprove of our own conduct, according as we feel that, when we place ourselves in the situation of another man, and view it, as it were, with his eyes and from his station, we either can or cannot entirely enter into and sympathize with the sentiments and motives which influenced it. (TMS III.1.1)

In judging oneself, one must try to divide oneself "as it were, into two persons": the "I" as agent or PPC, and the "I" who is judging the PPC (TMS III.1.6). Smith argues that the habit of judging one's own character in this way is what develops into what is often called one's "conscience." Now this may sound like a cumbersome process, but in practice it happens much more readily than it sounds. The idea is this: when you are reflecting on your own sentiments, you consider what another person informed of your situation would think. Would an impartial observer approve of your conduct? If so, then you may proceed; if not, then not.

But why should we care what an imaginary observer thinks of our conduct? For two reasons, Smith thinks. First, because your habit of doing so is so deeply ingrained in you already that if you do not heed your conscience you will be you unhappy. We can see the importance of this claim by recalling a classic problem in the history of philosophy. In the second book of Plato's *Republic*, Socrates is asked to respond to one of the most difficult and enduring problems in moral philosophy, namely: Why would a person not commit injustice if he could be absolutely certain he could get away with it? The question is prompted by the story of a young shepherd who discovers a ring with the magical power of making its wearer invisible. According to the story, the shepherd uses the ring's power of invisibility to commit adultery with his king's wife, then to conspire with her to surprise and murder the king, and finally to put himself upon the throne. The lesson of this story, according to Glaucon (who tells it), is that "one is never just willingly but only when compelled to be" (*Republic* II.360c).[14] Socrates thereupon commences a lengthy reply to this challenge, arguing ultimately that the life of injustice is not in fact more desirable than the life of justice: "And haven't we found that justice itself is the best thing for the soul itself, and that the soul— whether it has the ring of Gyges or even it together with the cap of Hades—should do just things?" (*Republic* X.612b). Socrates even suggests that the just person will fare better in the after-world than the unjust person—providing another reason to act justly in this life, even if one could act otherwise with impunity.[15]

The question of why one should be moral has persisted, how-ever, and Smith develops his own answer. According to Smith, man desires not only to be praised, but has a further desire "of being what he himself approves in other men" (TMS III.2.7). This further desire results, I believe,[16] from the continued workings of the desire for MSS. Here is how. All of us, Smith says, have at some time been frustrated or chagrined when people disapproved of our conduct because, we believe, they did not fully understand the circumstances involved. An only partial familiarity with another's situation might well bias or prejudice the judgment one makes, and probably all of us have experi-enced the unpleasantness of being on the wrong end of a biased, prejudiced, or partly uninformed (even misinformed) judgment. Smith argues that unpleasant experiences like these encourage us in such circumstances to repair, not to the judgment of actual observers' judgments, but instead to the judgment of an imaginary, informed, but disinterested observer. Smith calls this standard an "impartial spectator." And here we come to one of Smith's great contributions to moral philosophy: the concep-tion of the impartial spectator that constitutes the standard of morality.[17] Smith believes that this standard comes about naturally, or unintentionally, as a result on the one hand of individuals' wanting MSS and, on the other, their frequent frustration at others' inability or unwillingness to expend the effort that is sometimes necessary to come to understand another's full situation before passing judgment on his sentiments and actions. When mutual sympathy is not forthcoming from actual, and partial, spectators, we may find solace in an imagined impartial spectator who would approve of our conduct. Over time the practice of doing so becomes habitual, and so we will as often consult this imagined impartial spectator's sentiments as we will the sentiments of actual spectators.

Now we can see what Smith's answer is to Plato's Ring of Gyges problem. Even if we were guaranteed that no actual person would discover our misconduct, we would still be unable to avoid the damning judgment of our conscience, our imagined impartial spectator. This impartial spectator would inform us that our misconduct is such that we ourselves would condemn it in another person, and that realization is sufficient to trigger the antipathy, and thus displeasure, of a failure of MSS. "The man who has broke through all those measures of conduct, which can alone render him agreeable to mankind," Smith writes, when

> he looks back upon it, and views it in the light in which the impartial spectator would view it, he finds that he can enter into none of the motives which influenced it. He is abashed and confounded at the thoughts of it, and necessarily feels a very high degree of that shame which he would be exposed to, if his actions should ever come to be generally known. (TMS III.2.9)

The worse the misconduct, according to Smith, the greater the shame the person feels. If the misconduct is of the most grievous kinds, there is no escape from the judgment of the impartial spectator:

> These natural pangs of an affrighted conscience are the daemons, the avenging furies, which, in this life, haunt the guilty, which allow them neither quiet nor repose, which often drive them to despair and distraction, from which no assurance of secrecy can protect them, from which no principles of irreligion can entirely deliver them, and from which nothing can free them but the vilest and most abject of all states,

a complete insensibility to honour and infamy, to vice and virtue. (TMS III.2.9)[18]

The incentives one has to follow the rules of morality include, then: (1) the anticipated pleasure resulting from a MSS of actual spectators who approve of one's actions, and (2) the pleasure resulting from a sympathy of sentiments with an imagined impartial spectator; but also (3) the fear of an anticipated displeasure resulting from the judgment of other actual spectators who know of one's misdeed, and (4) the displeasure resulting from an antipathy of sentiments with an imagined impartial spectator. These conspire, Smith argues, to provide a powerful incentive to follow those rules of conduct that one approves in others and not to follow rules of conduct that one disapproves in others.

Thus the first reason Smith believes we should pay attention to what our conscience tells us is to avoid the substantial risk that we otherwise run of feeling unpleasant shame and disgrace at our own misconduct. The second reason is the other side of this equation: you are, or might be, able to achieve a pleasurable sympathy of sentiments with your imagined spectator. And the more thoroughly this imagined spectator knows the situations of your sentiments and conduct, and still approves, the more exquisite the pleasure you feel from the ensuing MSS. With diligence and application, a person can train himself, Smith thinks, to heed mainly, even perhaps exclusively, the judgment of the impartial spectator, and such a person will most nearly approximate the conduct of a truly virtuous person as a human being can:

> To a real wise man the judicious and well-weighed approba-
> tion of a single wise man, gives more heartfelt satisfaction
> than all the noisy applauses of ten thousand ignorant though
> enthusiastic admirers. He may say with Parmenides, who,
> upon reading a philosophical discourse before a public
> assembly at Athens, and observing, that, except Plato, the
> whole company had left him, continued, notwithstanding, to
> read on, and said that Plato alone was audience sufficient for
> him. (TMS VI.iii.31)[19]

Smith is adamant about this point. Unmerited applause brings no real pleasure, he insists, since we are always "secretly conscious"[20] to ourselves that we do not in fact merit the applause. At the same time, the pain we feel from unjust censure can sting more deeply and remain with us far longer than it should:

> Unmerited reproach, however, is frequently capable of mortifying very severely even men of more than ordinary constancy. [. . .] [A]n innocent man, though of more than ordinary constancy, is often, not only shocked, but most severely mortified by the serious, though false, imputation of a crime; especially when that imputation happens unfortunately to be supported by some circumstances which give it an air of probability. (TMS III.2.11)

Though such a person should repose and take comfort in the knowledge that an impartial spectator would not so condemn him, Smith allows that only people of the firmest "constancy" are capable of that kind of discipline.

But who exactly is this impartial spectator, and from where do his judgments come? What makes his judgments the "correct" ones, and wherein does this correctness consist? Are his judgments—or indeed *any* of the moral judgments to which people come, if Smith's account of their genealogy is correct—to be considered objectively true? Smith has given us an account of the origins of moral judgments that is based on the natural passions and sentiments in human beings, which suggests an unintentional, invisible-hand emergence of a larger order of morality from the more locally focused judgments of individuals in particular circumstances. Let us turn now to the questions of the moral status of judgments arrived at in this way.

Notes

1. Whether the changes in the successive editions of TMS are in fact significant is debated. For discussion, one might begin with the editors' introduction to the Glasgow Edition of TMS.
2. Like food and sex. See TMS II.i.5.10, II.ii.3.5, and VI.i.1.
3. See, for example, De Waal (2007), Ridley (1998) and E. O. Wilson (2004).
4. TMS I.ii.4.3 and I.iii.1.8.
5. WN I.iii and passim. For a more technical discussion of Smith's notion of markets, see Aspromourgos (2009), esp. chapters 3 and 4.

[6] Smith believes that other motivations may also be present in various circumstances; nevertheless "the desire of bettering our condition" is "a desire which, though generally calm and dispassionate, comes with us from the womb, and never leaves us till we go into the grave" (WN II.iii.28). See also WN I.viii.44, II.iii.31, II.iii.36, II.v.37, III.iii.12, IV.ii.4, IV.v.b.43, and IV.ix.28.

[7] See TMS I.i.2.1, I.i.3.4, I.i.4, and VII.iv.6.

[8] For a discussion of the *micro* and *macro* terminology and their function in explanations like these, see Schelling (1978).

[9] See, for example, TMS I.i.2.1, I.i.2.6, and I.i.3.1.

[10] Smith believes that this imaginative-switching-of-places explains everything from why a mother flies to her child when she hears its "moanings" from the "agony of disease" to how we can "sympathize even with the dead" to how we can sympathize with the plight of a person who has experienced "loss of reason." See TMS I.i.1.11–13.

[11] Smith does indeed believe there is such a thing as *justified resentment*. He even argues that there is such a thing as showing "too little spirit," by not taking proper action based on justified resentment (see, for example, TMS II.i.5.8 and VI.iii.16). Justified resentment plays an important role in Smith's conception of justice (and injustice), to which I return below.

[12] For an argument that Smith is, after all, trying to refine and improve our moral sentiments, albeit rather subtly, see Griswold (1999), esp. chapter 1.

[13] The phrase "invisible hand" does appear once in TMS, at IV.i.10, though in a somewhat different context.

[14] I use the Grube (1992) translation.

[15] Much of the *Republic* is an extended response to Glaucon's challenge. Socrates's suggestion that the just person will fare better in the afterworld is contained in his myth of Er, which begins at *Republic* X.614b.

[16] Other scholars have different views about the nature and origin of this desire. See, for example, Griswold (1999), chapter 3.

[17] The distinguished scholar D. D. Raphael (2007) has recently argued that this is Smith's most important and enduring contribution to moral philosophy.

[18] This passage sounds to me like an apt description of Raskolnikov in Dostoevsky's great *Crime and Punishment.*

[19] As the editors of the Glasgow edition of TMS note, the story Smith has in mind probably refers to Antimachus, not Parmenides. Parmenides probably died before Plato was born. See TMS VI.iii.31 n27.

[20] TMS III.4.12 and passim.

Chapter 4

The Impartial Spectator and Moral Objectivity

Adam Smith argues that human morality comprises a system of judgments that people in a given community make about the propriety or impropriety of the sentiments that lead to action and about the merit or demerit of the ends those actions propose. I suggested in Chapter 3 that Smith's account constitutes an "invisible-hand" argument, whereby individuals pursuing their own concerns—in this case, trying to achieve a "mutual sympathy of sentiments" (MSS) with the relevant actual or imagined agents—give rise to a larger system of moral order that benefits others as well. The benefit for others is that they can seek their own MSS within a background framework of rules, conventions, and protocols that have proved relatively effective at allowing others to achieve MSS. Hence each of us, in seeking his own MSS, makes it marginally easier for others to do the same; and since all of us are continually engaging in this pursuit, those habits and protocols that are less effective at producing MSS tend to disappear, while those that are more effective tend to endure. A community's longstanding moral rules would enjoy, then, a presumptive authority that others would be wise to adopt, at least until there is good reason to depart from them.

It would seem as if Smith's conception of human morality is a progressive one: making incremental steps ever closer to the, or an, ideal morality. Is that Smith's view? Perhaps, but only if everything were to go well—which it never does. We will explore later some of the ways the process can become corrupted. In this chapter, let us instead explore the moral status of the judgments arrived at in the seemingly material and almost mechanistic way Smith suggests. If this process results in the creation of an "impartial spectator" standard of morality, are there any reasons besides prudential ones to obey this standard? Is there any sense in which we can call this standard *right* or *correct*—not simply a contingent stratagem to allow us to get something we want?

The Solitary Man

In part III of *The Theory of Moral Sentiments* (TMS), Smith gives us an intriguing thought experiment: What sort of moral judgments would a person make, and what sort of moral sentiments would he have, if he grew up entirely alone? Now, this is a counterfactual thought experiment for Smith, since he believes humans are always in communities and that membership in groups, even only a family or tribe, is part of human nature: man "can subsist only in society," and nature "formed man for society" (TMS II. ii.3.1 and III.2.6, respectively). Still, if a person could grow up alone, what morality would he have? Smith's answer:

> Were it possible that a human creature could grow up to manhood in some solitary place, without any communication with his own species, he could no more think of his own character, of the propriety or demerit of his own sentiments and conduct, of the beauty or deformity of his own mind, than of the beauty or deformity of his own face. (TMS III.1.3)

He might have a sense of what things in his environment conduced to his ends and what did not—whether things "pleased or hurt him" (ibid.)—but no sense of propriety or impropriety of his own behavior. Why not? The answer is suggested by the continuation of the thought experiment: "Bring him into society, and he is immediately provided with the mirror which he wanted before" (ibid.). What the solitary man lacked while in isolation, then, is experiencing the judgment of others, which makes him confront his own behavior: this is the social "mirror" to which Smith refers. Once he is in "society" with other humans and thus experiences their (sometimes negative) judgments, his formerly latent desire for MSS is triggered, beginning the gradual process of developing moral sentiments.

This thought experiment provides the two key elements indicating what moral objectivity Smith thinks our moral judgments enjoy: (1) moral judgments are the products of rules that develop and unfold, and are not eternally fixed or handed down from on high; (2) they originate from and depend upon human "society" and interaction. Take the process of development first. Smith repeatedly describes the sentiments of morality as unfolding according to a process of negative and positive feedback dependent upon whether a person does or does not achieve MSS. Referring again to the solitary man, Smith writes:

> Bring him into society, and all his own passions will immediately become the cause of new passions. He will observe that mankind approve of some of them, and are disgusted by others. He will be elevated in the one case, and cast down in the other; his desires and aversions, his joys and sorrows, will now often become the cause of new desires and new aversions, new joys and new sorrows: they will now, therefore, interest him deeply, and often call upon his most attentive consideration. (TMS III.1.3)

Smith here recapitulates the process through which he believes all humans normally go when they transition slowly from infants with no sense of moral propriety to adults with a complicated and delicate sense of moral propriety. The precise moment in that process described here—when the solitary man is brought "into society"—is the moment Smith elsewhere describes as normally occurring to children when they first go to play with their mates and thus enter "the great school of self-command" (TMS III.3.22).[1]

The mutual adjustment of sentiments and behavior that begin upon this first experience of being judged by others leads in time to the development of habits and conventions of behavior, and then to "general rules of morality."

> It is thus that the general rules of morality are formed. They are ultimately founded upon experience of what, in particular instances, our moral faculties, our natural sense of merit and propriety, approve, or disapprove of. [. . .] The general rule [. . .] is formed, by finding from experience, that all actions of a certain kind, or circumstanced in a certain manner, are approved or disapproved of. (TMS III.4.8)

Note the repeated emphasis on *experience*. There is no way, Smith believes, for a person to come to moral judgments other than by relying on his experience of what actually and in fact he, and

others, approve or disapprove in others. Nor is this necessary
reliance on past experience limited to our judgments of others:
it is what generates the perspective of the impartial spectator by
which we judge ourselves as well. When judging our own conduct, we thus engage in a kind of moral triangulation. When we
behave in a certain way toward another person, we have not two
but three perspectives to consider:

> We must view [our sentiments], neither from our own place
> nor yet from his [i.e., the object of our actions], but from the
> place and with the eyes of a third person, who has no particu-
> lar connexion with either, and who judges with impartiality
> between us. (TMS III.3.3)

How, in practice, does Smith think we are able to accomplish
this feat of triangulation? Past experience yet again: "habit and
experience have taught us to do this so easily and so readily, that
we are scarce sensible that we do it" (ibid.). Smith's argument,
then, is not that there are no standards: clearly there are. Instead,
he believes that the standards arise from "habit and experience,"
not from apprehension of first principles, and they are prag-
matically oriented toward the actual purposes and experiences
people have.

But are they *right*? Is there reason to think that we ought to
obey them, ought to credit them, or ought to endorse them,
apart from their apparent localized historical imprimatur?
Smith's standard of morality is the impartial spectator, but if this
imaginary personage is simply the coalescence of our inductively
arrived-at generalizations based on our past contingent experiences of what sentiments and behaviors have met with approval,
then is this viewpoint not simply a creature of the particular
place and time in which one lives? Can moral standards such as
these have any claim to objectivity?

Moral Rules and "Middle-way" Objectivity

Smith's contemporary Thomas Reid (1710–96) said that on
Hume's view all a judge is supposed to do is observe the facts,
and, once he has done so: "Nothing remains, on his part, but to
feel the right or the wrong; and mankind have, very absurdly,

called him a *judge*, he ought to be called a *feeler*."[2] This was meant as a *reductio ad absurdum* of Hume's view: obviously, Reid thought, to be a judge, one must *judge*, not merely *feel*. This was an abiding worry about basing moral judgments on "sentiments." But whether or not Reid's is a valid objection to Hume, Smith's position would not fall prey to the same objection—though one would be forgiven for initially suspecting as much. For Smith, the rendering of the moral judgment includes a deduction from principles, not a mere "feeling" of the right or wrong. The moral principles are those general rules that one has developed over time on the basis of one's experience with the results of various methods of attempting to achieve MSS in various kinds of circumstances.

In the process of passing an actual judgment, what one does, according to Smith, is consult the relevant general rules, ask whether the sentiment or behavior one is judging comports with those rules, and thereby deduces whether the sentiment or behavior should be approved or not. Such a deduction approximates the following form:

Step 1: We observe that a "stranger passes by us in the street with all the marks of the deepest affliction" (TMS I.i.3.4).
Step 2: We apply the general rule that, unless there are special circumstances, a person should not carry on like that in public.
Step 3: We realize that there are no special circumstances in this case.
Step 4: We therefore disapprove of his behavior.

Suppose, however, that "we are immediately told that he [the stranger] has just received the news of the death of his father" (ibid.). Now the deduction changes, because we realize that special circumstances do obtain. The new deduction takes this form:

Step 1': Same as Step 1.
Step 2': Same as Step 2.
Step 3': Now realizing that this is a special circumstance, we apply a new rule based on the nature of the special circumstance in question: People who recently learned

of the death of a close relative are given far more
latitude to express their emotions, even publicly.

Step 4': This stranger's public display falls within the proper
scope.

Step 5': It is therefore now "impossible that, in this case, we
should not approve of his grief" (TMS I.i.3.4).

This is the procedure that Smith believes actually results in the
passing of moral judgments. Its reliance on intersubjectively
generated moral rules absolves it from the charge that it is the
result of mere "feeling" or subject to the whims and fluctuations
of our emotions. But the question remains whether these moral
standards have any further foundation beyond contingent
subjective experience.

The moral standards that arise in the way Smith describes are
what philosopher John Searle calls "institutional facts," which "are
portions of the real world, objective facts in the world, that
are facts only by human agreement" (Searle 1997: 1). Unlike, say,
rocks and trees, these standards have no physical existence; they
are, using Searle's terminology, *ontologically subjective*, meaning that
their existence depends on the beliefs and attitudes of particular
agents. On the other hand, they are *epistemically objective*, meaning
that it is not simply a matter of any single person's opinion whether
they exist or not or what their basic features are: their existence
and nature are rather a matter of objectively ascertainable fact.
An example will illustrate. It either is or is not the case that polygamy is morally objectionable in your community. It is not objectionable in Saudi Arabia, though it is objectionable in Selma,
Alabama.[3] Your opinion about polygamy is irrelevant to that fact,
in the same way that your opinion about what a baseball auto-
graphed by Babe Ruth is *really* worth is irrelevant to the fact that
one might fetch several thousand dollars at an auction.

This is what I propose to call the "middle-way" objectivity that
Smithian moral standards enjoy. They are not directly dependent on any transcendent, otherworldly sanction, like God or
Natural Law, and yet they are neither arbitrary nor dependent
on any person's individual opinion. They are objective in that
they are facts of our social reality. This objectivity arises in virtue
of the fact that they are the result of the invisible-hand process
of local (micro) intentions creating general (macro) order.
It also arises because, as I have suggested, the shared standards

rely on and develop in consequence of certain features of our common human nature—in particular our desire for MSS. A community's moral standards will, Smith says, vary along less important themes—protocols of clothing, for example, forms of greeting and address, and so on.[4] Thus the complete description of any given community's shared system of morality will, owing to the community's unique historical station, be itself unique. Nonetheless certain rules will almost, perhaps in fact, invariably obtain because of our shared humanity: for example, rules against murder of innocents (properly described), against incest (properly qualified), recommending hospitality and reciprocity (under proper circumstances), and so on.

If Smith is asked why one should follow the moral rules of one's community, he would give several reasons. First, because doing so gives you the best chance of achieving something that you greatly desire, namely MSS. Hence it is in your own interest to do so. Second, because that is what others expect of you, and insofar as you care about their chances of achieving mutual sympathy you should increase those chances by doing what is expected of you. And you do care about others—recall the opening sentence of TMS:

> How selfish soever man may be supposed, there are evidently some principles in his nature, which interest him in the fortune of others, and render their happiness necessary to him, though he derives nothing from it except the pleasure of seeing it. (TMS I.i.1.1)

Third and finally, you should follow the moral rules of your community because it is one key to happiness. Smith believes that a principal constituent of happiness is loving and intimate relations with others: "the chief part of human happiness arises from the consciousness of being beloved" (TMS I.ii.5.1); he asks, "What so great happiness as to be beloved, and to know that we deserve to be beloved?" (TMS III.1.7). The way we become "beloved" is by spending time with others whom we love and by behaving in ways that we know will inspire and encourage their love. Acting virtuously, or according to the dictates of the impartial spectator, or according to the general rules of morality we have developed, is, according to Smith, perhaps the "surest way" to achieving happiness.

No benevolent man ever lost altogether the fruits of his benevolence. If he does not always gather them from the persons from he ought to have gathered them, he seldom fails to gather them, and with a tenfold increase, from other people. Kindness is the parent of kindness; and if to be beloved by our brethren be the great object of our ambition, the surest way of obtaining it is, by our conduct to show that we really love them. (TMS VI.ii.1.19)

Happiness, then, attends upon being beloved, which itself attends both upon close and familiar relationships with others and upon our behaving in ways that we know they would, or should, approve—that is, upon the consciousness of being worthy of being beloved.

We therefore have another reason to follow the dictates of the impartial spectator and the general rules of morality that inform his judgment, namely because doing so increases the chances of being happy. This constitutes a hypothetical imperative: if you want to be happy, you should for the most part follow the moral standards of your community. The "for the most part" is an important qualification. Since the moral standards arise on the basis of a market-like process, innovation—entrepreneurship—is an integral element. Hence novel, abnormal, and unexpected behaviors will be part and parcel of its living quality; that is a large part of what makes these systems of order turbulent at the micro-level. The trick for an entrepreneur, of course, is to know when innovation will succeed and when it will not, when trying something new would be approved and when not, and what kinds of new things might appropriately be attempted and what not. Successful moral entrepreneurs—"success" meaning achieving MSS —are those who know or can anticipate such things, just as successful economic entrepreneurs are those who successfully answer analogous questions in economic marketplaces. Many entrepreneurial ventures in morality will fail, but some will not; the latter may lead to changes at the margins that over time may recast some elements of a given community's system of morality.

One might object here that although polygamy, to return to our earlier example, is *considered* objectionable in one place and *considered* unobjectionable in another, it does not follow from this that polygamy is *in fact* objectionable or not. Polygamy might be objectionable or not quite independently of what any community believes about it. On Smith's account, however, it seems it is not possible to make any such independent or transcendent judgment, since we lack the grounds to do so. One might claim that one finds polygamy distasteful, that one believes it has baleful consequences, that one wishes that more people in one's community reacted to it the way oneself does, that it conflicts with one's religious views or other moral commitments, and so on. But none of these would change the fact that the practice is in fact judged to be whatever it is judged to be by one's community's moral standards. On Smith's account, moral standards are created by the market-like mechanism I have described, so there is no inherent or intrinsic rightness or wrongness about them. However we might like to think they enjoy some privileged or special status, our own moral intuitions and traditions too are informed by this same mechanism, just as are those of people whose intuitions and traditions run differently. Now, the actual consequences of practices like polygamy are empirically ascertainable, and that could anchor an objective moral judgment based on a broadly utilitarian premise. But the judgment would again be hypothetical—something like: given your circumstances and your nature, if you want to be happy, you should do *x*. On the Smithian account we lack the tools required to make categorical moral judgments.

Yet Smith might believe that moral judgments could enjoy a sanction beyond what a strict market mechanism would provide, based on his beliefs about the origins of the fixed elements of human nature and the way they function in moral orders. TMS is replete with mentions of God, Nature (capital "n"), the Author of Nature, and so on, and Smith's belief, apparently, is that this Intelligence designed human nature in such a way that "natural" human behavior can (unintentionally) give rise to systems of order that are beneficial. This suggests that the moral judgments arising by means of the market mechanism might ultimately, if by an indirect route, have been intended by God: How else could one explain the presence of the necessary fixed elements of human nature, in particular the desire for the MSS?[5] It is crucial to see, however, that such divine sanction would not necessarily justify any particular individual judgment or action. Rather, it would lend its imprimatur only to the overall, or macro-, system, which is what Smith argues conduces to human benefit. Thus although Smith might say that the properly formed moral system is conducive to human welfare and, because God intends human welfare, must therefore itself be intended by God, nevertheless there is no way to know in advance, from intuition or from *a priori* analysis, whether any particular judgment is justified in this way. One could only make the tentative *ex post* judgment that if people flourish under it, then the system might be intended by God. Although, then, this might be considered a transcendent sanction after a fashion, it is a rather weak one, not least because it has little predictive value. Moreover, Smith's view here may speak more to his own peculiar religious views than to the way the market mechanism he is describing functions.

Utility

Yet Smith's account does suggest a more general criterion by which one can judge one's own moral system or that of other communities: utility. Even if Smith's account allows nothing intrinsically right or wrong about the judgments sanctioned by one's system of morality, nonetheless, as I suggested, one can take empirical stock of its relative beneficial or harmful effects on people's wellbeing, and praise or condemn it accordingly on those grounds. We need not ascribe to Smith the idea that what is involved is an exact mathematical calculation or a summing of individual utility functions, something perhaps impossible to do in any case.[6] But Smith does seem to believe that an objectively testable empirical judgment can be formed about whether a given set of rules conduces to or does not conduce to people's wellbeing.[7] Again, because of the way Smith thinks the market mechanism works, his expectation is that the systems of order produced will tend overall and in the long run to be beneficial rather than harmful. Because each person is always acting to better his own condition, the rules of behavior and judgment that the community develops will tend to be conducive to everyone's benefit. There are many ways that this process can be corrupted, of course, as Smith is well aware. But Smith's argument is addressing of long-run tendencies.[8]

The role Smith ascribes to utility in morality is more complicated, however, than this brief description would suggest. Early in TMS, Smith writes, "Philosophers have, of late years"—he is probably thinking of Hume—

considered chiefly the tendency of affections, and have given little attention to the relation which they stand in to the cause which excites them. In common life, however, when we judge of any person's conduct, and of the sentiments which directed it, we constantly consider them under both these aspects. (TMS I.i.3.8)

Both aspects—utility and propriety—are part of a complete moral judgment for Smith, as we saw in Chapter 3. Alluding again to Hume, Smith continues,

The utility of those qualities [viz., the intellectual virtues], it may be thought, is what first recommends them to us; and, no doubt, the consideration of this, when we come to attend to it, gives them a new value. Originally, however, we approve of another man's judgment, not as something useful, but as right, as accurate, as agreeable to truth and reality. (TMS I.i.4.4)

This passage contains the complication in Smith's conception of the role of utility, because it describes not one but two levels of explanation for a moral judgment—and the two levels are easily confused. The first level is the deduction from the applicable general moral rule of approval or disapproval, as described earlier. It is this level that Smith here describes as what one does "originally," and a sentiment's or behavior's comportment with the relevant rule(s) is, I suggest, what he refers to here "as right, as accurate, as agreeable to truth and reality." A sentiment's being approved as proper under the relevant rule(s) just is, for Smith, what it means for a sentiment to be morally right.

There is, however, a second level of explanation as well, namely the explanation of the origin of the general rules themselves. As shown earlier, they arise on the basis of an imperfect market-like process that winnows and culls, tending to keep and discard rules based on their continuing relative success at achieving MSS. When Smith writes that the "idea of the utility of all qualities of this kind, is plainly an after-thought, and not what first recommends them to our approbation" (TMS I.i.4.4), he means that the first level of explanation—the deduction—takes place without any conscious reference to utility. He does not mean to suggest, however, that utility is irrelevant to all levels of explanation or to the entire process. Smith recognizes the role of utility in the second level of explanation. Consider, for example, his discussion of "the young and the licentious" whom we hear "ridiculing the most sacred rules of morality, and professing, sometimes from the corruption, but more frequently from the vanity of their hearts, the most abominable maxims of conduct" (TMS II.ii.3.8). We naturally get upset at this, Smith says, and our first thought is to appeal to these young profligates with the "intrinsic hatefulness and detestableness" of their sentiments; when they dispute that, however, Smith says "we generally cast about for other arguments, and the consideration that [next] occurs to us, is the disorder and confusion of society which would result from the universal prevalence of such practices" (ibid.). Smith continues:

> But though it commonly requires no great discernment to see the destructive tendency of all licentious practices to the welfare of society, it is seldom this consideration which first animates us against them. All men, even the most stupid and unthinking, abhor fraud, perfidy, and injustice, and delight to see them punished. But few men have reflected upon the necessity of justice to the existence of society, how obvious soever that necessity may appear to be. (TMS II.ii.3.9)

"How obvious soever that necessity may appear to be . . ." to the *philosopher*, we can almost hear Smith continuing. Hume had argued that utility forms the chief part of our regard for all virtues, and the sole part for many of them.[9] Here Smith acknowledges that a brilliant philosopher like Hume[10] is able, perhaps, to reconstruct the chain that links the sentiments we approve to our own, others', or society's utility. But his suggestion is that many people do not, or even cannot, reconstruct that complicated chain, and thus few if any people have any such notions in mind when they actually pass a moral judgment. Coming to realize the utility of an action can make it appear more beautiful, Smith says; "This beauty, however, is chiefly perceived by men of reflection and speculation, and is by no means the quality which first recommends such actions to the natural sentiments of the bulk of mankind" (TMS IV.2.11). Instead, mankind thinks of what is "right," not what conduces to utility.

Smith devotes an entire part of TMS (part IV) to exploring what effect utility has on our sentiments of approbation, and his discussion there gives him an opportunity to introduce what he can justly claim is probably his own discovery. He begins by again acknowledging the force of Hume's position: "The utility of any object, according to him [Hume], pleases the master by perpetually suggesting to him the pleasure or conveniency which it is fitted to promote" (TMS IV.1.2). "But," Smith counters,

> this fitness, this happy contrivance of any production of art, should often be more valued, than the very end for which it was intended; and that the exact adjustment of the means for attaining any conveniency or pleasure, should frequently be more regarded, than the very conveniency or pleasure, in the attainment of which their whole merit would seem to consist, has not, so far as I know, been yet taken notice of by any body. (TMS IV.1.3)

Smith's discussion here parallels the two-level explanation he gives of moral judgments. In these passages, Smith recognizes two separate elements giving rise to the judgment: the actual utility that a "contrivance" or "production of art" provides, and, separately, the relative "fitness" between the contrivance and the end it is designed to serve. The latter is like the first or initial judgment one passes on a sentiment—whether it is "right" or not, whether it is proper or not, in itself. Smith suggests that a well-constructed pocket-watch would give rise to this kind of approbation. On the other hand, the former element is like the second level, often left unpursued, of the way in which what strikes one as right or proper in fact conduces to utility. The actual cost to utility of a watch that loses a few minutes per day, Smith suggests, is not worth the extra money it costs to buy a more accurate timepiece, yet people will spend the money anyway (TMS IV.1.5). The reason: people like the idea of its precision more than the utility it might serve. Smith says that people will indeed "ruin themselves by laying out money on trinkets of frivolous utility" (TMS IV.1.6)—which he takes as proof that utility cannot be the only thing they care about.

Utility often does not, then, inform the immediate judgment people make about watches—or about sentiments or behaviors. Instead it is the watch's adherence to their notions of fitness, or the sentiment's or behavior's adherence to the applicable general rule. In the moral arena, awareness of a sentiment's or behavior's conduciveness toward utility can amplify or diminish the initial judgment, as the case may be, but it does not constitute the judgment. On the other hand, a sentiment or behavior that leads to an increase in utility—which will often consist largely in a MSS—tends to reinforce the sentiment or behavior and may ultimately establish a rule that will inform future judgments. When, therefore, Smith writes "But still I affirm, that it is not the view of this utility or hurtfulness which is either the first or principal source of our approbation and disapprobation" (TMS IV.2.3), he is referring to the first level of moral judgment noted above. The rules applied at this level are themselves based in utility, though we often, perhaps usually, do not realize it. Thus the Smithian moral judgment relies on an objective utility, and his moral theory, like his economic theory, is ultimately informed by utility. This provides it an empirical, pragmatic process of justification, if not a direct transcendent justification.

How High Does the Impartial Spectator Go?

The explanation Smith gives for the creation of the impartial spectator's viewpoint indicates that it too enjoys a "middle-way" objectivity: not subject to the whim of any individual, yet not eternal or transcendent. It is dependent on the inductive generalizations each of us makes on his own experience of interacting with others and the norms we develop through negotiation with one another. Its authority would be presumptive and conditional, but neither impotent nor arbitrary. Yet Smith sometimes speaks of this perspective as though it has a rather more elevated status—as, for example, when he refers to the impartial spectator as "this demigod within the breast" that is "partly of immortal, yet partly too of mortal extraction" (TMS III.2.32). In the first editions of TMS, Smith called the impartial spectator a "vicegerent upon earth," an "inmate of the breast, this abstract man, the representative of mankind, and substitute of the Deity" (TMS III.2.31, note r). How does this elevated language square with the terrestrial image I have painted of Smith's impartial spectator?

It pertains, first, to a psychological claim Smith is making. Smith argues that the greater the bearing any given protocol, habit, or general moral rule has on the relevant community's survival, the more frequently will its observance be noted, remarked, and insisted upon by the members of that community, and thus the more strongly will the impartial spectator approve following it and condemn disobeying it. The rigors of reality discipline us, as it were, to seek out and observe good behaviors. As we have seen, this will not, according to Smith, be a conscious process of gradation according to utility; rather, it will come about spontaneously, through trial and error, by repetition and reinforcement. For a handful of rules—which Smith will designate the rules of "justice"—their connection to a community's survival is so close and so immediate that the impartial spectator insists upon them. Smith argues there are but three rules of "justice":

> The most sacred laws of justice, therefore, those whose violation seems to call loudest for vengeance and punishment, are [1] the laws which guard the life and person of our neighbour; [2] the next are those which guard his property and possessions; and [3] last of all come those which guard what are called his personal rights, or what is due to him from the promises of others. (TMS II.ii.2.2)

The observance of these rules of justice constitute "the foundation which supports the building" of society, "the main pillar that upholds the whole edifice" (TMS II.ii.3.4). They are so important to a society's survival that even a "society among robbers and murders" must respect them with one another (TMS II.ii.3.3). Because of their supreme importance to a society's survival, the impartial spectator's perspective we generate comes to approve of their observance in all circumstances, and approve of their punishment in all breaches.

Smith's occasionally elevated language in describing the impartial spectator pertains to a second claim as well. Smith writes:

> When the general rules which determine the merit and demerit of actions, come thus to be regarded as the laws of an All-powerful Being, who watches over our conduct, and who, in a life to come, will reward the observance, and punish the breach of them; they necessarily acquire a new sacredness from this consideration. (TMS III.5.12)

This again is a psychological observation Smith is making, not something he is endorsing or condemning: people are more likely to follow rules of behavior if they think those rules trace to the will of a divine god. Because of this, Smith argues, some general rules—namely those whose observance are most crucial to the survival of the society—come, as Smith puts it, to be "justly regarded as the Laws of the Deity" (TMS III.5.1). Note that he does not say they *are* the laws of the deity, only that they are justly *regarded* as such. His argument here is consistent with the explanation of the impartial spectator's perspective given earlier in this chapter. Any parent can attest to the effectiveness of telling a child that she must obey the rule in question because God is watching her and will know if she broke His rule. Whether God in fact is watching, and whether in fact this rule is God's rule, is irrelevant. What matters is that the child regards the rule to be God's, and many a parent, I daresay, has adverted to such an expedient when trying to raise the probability that a child will observe important rules of conduct.

Smith writes that "It is in this manner that religion enforces the natural sense of duty" (TMS III.5.13). My argument is that the dynamic he believes he has discovered explaining the natural—if unintentional or "spontaneous"—progression from "desired conduct *x*" to "God commands *x*" parallels the mechanism involved in our sense that the impartial spectator's perspective is or can be a "substitute of the Deity." Because of the importance to society's survival of its observance of, for example, the rules of justice, many societies hit upon the device of propagating a belief in their direct connection to God's will. For similar reasons, many societies have discovered and pursued the device of propagating a belief that the impartial spectator is one's "guardian angel" (in more modern parlance), or God's "vicegerent upon earth" (in Smith's language). It turns out, then, that this imagined person's perspective is nothing metaphysical or otherwise mysterious, and, as is typical for Smith, he is able to account for his existence by using the explanatory principles he has already developed.

One more note on this score. Smith writes that the general rules of morality are "justly regarded as the Laws of the Deity" (TMS III.5.1), and in the interpretation I have just given I put the emphasis on the word "regarded," not on the word "justly." One might, however, wish to emphasize "justly," taking it to mean "truly," "accurately," or "correctly," in which case one might take this line as suggestive of Smith's own religious views. I acknowledge the plausibility of this interpretation, even if it is not mine. Later in the same chapter, while discussing whether people are capable of "acting upon all occasions with the most delicate and accurate propriety," Smith answers, "The coarse clay of which the bulk of mankind are formed, cannot be wrought up to such perfection" (TMS III.5.1). Though no one is perfect, nevertheless "any man" can, "by discipline, education, and example," learn to "act upon almost every occasion with tolerable decency, and through the whole of his life to avoid any considerable degree of blame" (TMS III.5.1). I believe that this is the kind of position a Smithian, if you will pardon the expression, should take. As Smith wrote in a 1759 letter,

> The Great judge of the World, has, for the wisest reasons, thought proper to interpose, between the weak eye of human reason and the throne of his eternal justice, a degree of obscurity and darkness which, tho it does not entirely cover that great tribunal from the view of mankind, yet renders the impression of it faint and feeble in comparison of what might be expected from the grandeur and importance of so mighty an object. (C, 53)

Yet Smith continues:

> That men, however, might never be without a rule to direct their conduct by, nor without a judge whose authority should enforce its observation, the author of nature has made man the immediate judge of mankind, and has, in this respect, as in many others, created him after his own image, and appointed him his vicegerent upon earth to Superintend the behaviour of his brethren. They are taught by Nature to acknowledge that power and jurisdiction which has thus been confered upon him, and to tremble or exult according as they imagine that they have either merited his Censure or deserved his Applause. (C, 53)

We are imperfect creatures, but we are capable of improving ourselves; similarly, our standard of morality—the perspective of the impartial spectator—will in practice reflect the errors and biases to which we imperfect creatures are prone, but it nevertheless can be improved by experience. Smith may believe that the development and gradual improvement of the self-enforced standard of an impartial spectator is progress intended by God and encouraged by the human nature and human circumstances

He created. Whether in fact this was, as Smith perhaps suggests, God's intention, Smith does believe that the process itself takes place and is the correct explanation for both the moral standards human beings develop and for the "sacred" regard they accord to some of them.[11]

How Good a Standard is the Impartial Spectator?

I close this chapter by raising, but forgoing discussion of, the question of whether employing an imagined perspective of an impartial spectator can actually be a reliable guide to proper conduct. This question is impossible to answer here. Yet perhaps I might ask you, dear reader, a question. The next time you face a quandary or dilemma, if you took a moment to ask yourself— literally ask yourself, and imagine an answer to—whether an informed but disinterested observer of your conduct would approve of what you are contemplating, would that supply some clarity? Perhaps two examples will suggest that Smith was on to something.

First, there has been a recurring fashion among some Christians, a fashion that recently resurfaced in the southern United States, for people to wear bracelets, shirts, or other items emblazoned with the letters "WWJD." It stands for the question "What would Jesus do?" Its point is to remind the wearer to take a moment's reflection to ask whether this particular observer— Jesus—would approve of the wearer's conduct. Second, Smith's conception of the impartial spectator as the ultimate arbiter of propriety and merit bears a resemblance to Aristotle's *phronemos*, or "virtuous man." In his *Nicomachean Ethics*, Aristotle argues that practical reason, when functioning rightly, issues in the perspective of a "virtuous man," and a good device for determining whether what one is contemplating doing is virtuous or vicious is to ask oneself what a truly virtuous person would do in one's situation. The person who occupies, in one's imagination, the personage of this "truly virtuous person" may vary from one individual to the next: perhaps a statesman, perhaps a wise relative or friend, perhaps the Son of God. Aristotle does not give a genealogical account of his "virtuous man," however, which leaves the question open for him what exactly the source of his authority is. Smith's genealogy of the impartial spectator might thus be an attempt to fill this lacuna in the theory. Regardless, these examples, I think Smith would say, are perfectly explicable on his analysis, and the effectiveness that these exemplars, and others like them, have at offering relatively, if not absolutely, reliable guides for good conduct constitutes *prima facie* evidence in support of his analysis. They may also help us become better people, which is a happy, if secondary, result of the analysis.

Notes

1 Smith summarizes this process in an abbreviated, but arguably clearer, way in a crucial letter to Gilbert Elliot dated October 10, 1759 (C, 48–57; see esp. 54–5).
2 Reid (1991 [1788]), 305.
3 I take this example from Hocutt (2000), 10–11.
4 See TMS V.2.1 and V.2.7–8.
5 Smith also argued that a community's longstanding moral rules would come to be seen by its members as their moral duty, and perhaps also as the will of God (see TMS III.5), but that is a descriptive claim and not part of the argument grounding normativity. See Kleer (1995).
6 See Otteson (2006), chapter 4.
7 Samuel Fleischacker interprets Smith quite differently from the way I do; he writes, for example, "Smith's moral theory is deeply opposed to utilitarianism" (Fleischacker 2005: 47).
8 Scholars disagree about whether Smith was ultimately an optimist or a pessimist about such "natural" systems of order. I believe he was a qualified optimist: too much of a realist to believe that everything always worked out for the better, but nevertheless confident about humankind's long-run chances of achieving beneficial social orders. See Alvey (2003) and Brubaker (2006).
9 See, for example, Hume (2006 [1751]), esp. chapter 5.
10 Smith says Hume is "an ingenious and agreeable philosopher, who joins the greatest depth of thought to the greatest elegance of expression, and possesses the singular and happy talent of treating the abstrusest subjects not only with the most perfect perspicuity, but with the most lively eloquence" (TMS IV.1.2).
11 I leave unresolved the issue of whether Smith believed that this was God's intention, whether indeed he believed in God, what his religious beliefs were, and so on, because I view such questions as necessarily dependent upon speculation. But the issue has been frequently discussed by scholars. See, for example, Denis (2005), Haakonssen (2006), and Minowitz (1993). See also Oslington (forthcoming).

Chapter 5

Political Economy in *The Theory of Moral Sentiments*

"Political economy" is the term that arose in the eighteenth century to describe the kind of studies in which Smith engaged— investigations into the political, economic, and other social institutions that affect human prosperity. In Scotland, political economy had been a standard part of the curriculum of what was called "moral philosophy" even earlier than the eighteenth century, but Smith carried on the tradition of his teacher Francis Hutcheson (and of Hutcheson's teacher, Gershom Carmichael [1672–1729], who was the first Professor of Moral Philosophy in Scotland), in his lectures at the University of Glasgow. The bulk of Smith's contributions to this field is contained in his *Wealth of Nations* (WN), but there is substantial material elsewhere. For example, although Smith did not publish them himself, two sets of students' notes of his lectures on jurisprudence, which he delivered for years at Glasgow, survive and have now been collected and published. There is also what scholars refer to as an "early draft" of some aspects of the WN, which is a manuscript of some 20 pages on "the nature and causes of public opulence" written probably in early 1763.[1] Finally, what might surprise the modern reader, there is considerable attention to political economy in Smith's *Theory of Moral Sentiments* (TMS) as well.[2]

Let us, then, investigate the main principles of Smith's political economy, starting, where Smith did, with TMS. One question to keep in mind as we proceed is in what school or tradition of political and economic thought Smith rightly belongs. This question is relevant not only because the existence of this book in a series entitled "Major Conservative and Libertarian Thinkers" already makes a claim in this regard, but also because this is a contested issue among scholars. I will state my own position in due course, but Smith's work is rich and sophisticated enough to allow more than one good-faith interpretation.

As I argued in Chapter 3, Smith's main task in TMS is to describe the mechanism that leads to individuals adopting moral codes and to communities developing shared moral codes. It was first published in 1759, when Smith was a young 36 years old, and, though he had been giving the lectures on which TMS was based for several years, it contains, as one might expect, some youthful flourishes among its brilliant insights. The periodic discussions that we would now recognize as political economy rather than moral theory contain elements of both.

In this short chapter, let us focus on three main aspects of Smith's political economy in TMS: (1) his conception of happiness; (2) his distinction between justice and beneficence; and (3) his intriguing discussion of the "man of system."

Happiness

In TMS, Smith seems to think that the main part of happiness consists in a kind of tranquility, not unlike the Stoical *apatheia* or indifference toward the vicissitudes of life.[3] "Happiness consists in tranquillity and enjoyment. Without tranquillity there can be no enjoyment; and where there is perfect tranquillity there is scarce anything which is not capable of amusing" (TMS III.3.30). In the next few paragraphs following that passage Smith goes on to mention "tranquillity" nearly a dozen times. Earlier in TMS he had written,

> Hatred and anger are the greatest poison to the happiness of a good mind. There is, in the very feeling of those passions, something harsh, jarring, and convulsive, something that tears and distracts the breast, and is altogether destructive of that composure and tranquillity of mind which is so necessary to happiness, and which is best promoted by the contrary passions of gratitude and love. (I.ii.3.7)

These two passages suggest that although happiness is not identical to tranquility, nevertheless tranquility is necessary for happiness, and nearly, though not quite, sufficient. What is also required is "enjoyment" (according to the first passage quoted above) or "gratitude and love" (second passage). In another place, Smith writes this: "What can be added to the happiness of the man who is in health, who is out of debt, and who has a clear conscience?" (TMS I.iii.1.7). This passage might sound as if it is introducing other elements necessary for happiness, but upon reconsideration I think its claim is that the opposite of the three things he lists—that is, bad health, debt, and a guilty conscience—are the three principal causes of mental unrest and turmoil; thus removing them paves the way for the tranquility he has been discussing.

To emphasize the point, Smith elsewhere offers one of his perhaps youthful rhetorical flourishes. He writes,

> In what constitutes the real happiness of human life, [the poor] are in no respect inferior to those who would seem so much above them. In ease of body and peace of mind, all the different ranks of life are nearly upon a level, and the beggar, who suns himself by the side of the highway, possesses that security which kings are fighting for. (TMS IV.1.11)

The end of this passage strikes the modern ear somewhat discordantly. Can Smith be serious in suggesting that the beggar's life is more tranquil—and thus, apparently, happier—than that of kings? Yet Smith gives another story that has, apparently, the same moral:

> What the favourite of the king of Epirus said to his master, may be applied to men in all the ordinary situations of life. When the king had recounted to him, in their proper order, all the conquests which he proposed to make, and had come to the last of them; And what does your Majesty propose to do then? said the Favourite.—I propose then, said the King, to enjoy myself with my friends, and endeavour to be good company over a bottle.—And what hinders your Majesty from doing so now? replied the Favourite. (TMS III.3.31)

In this case, Smith draws the lesson explicitly for us:

> In the most glittering and exalted situation that our idle fancy can hold out to us, the pleasures from which we propose to derive our real happiness, are always almost the same with

those which, in our actual, though humble station, we have at all times at hand, and in our power. (ibid.)

I think the conception of happiness Smith offers in the WN is somewhat different from TMS's conception, and I will argue in Chapter 8 that the idea that happiness consists in tranquility is almost certainly wrong. But in TMS Smith takes this view seriously, and it informs a rather dramatic parable he tells about a "poor man's son" (TMS IV.i.8). Heaven, Smith tells us, has visited this sorry soul with ambition: upon seeing how well appointed are the homes of the rich, he becomes dissatisfied with his father's cottage, and so he submits himself to a regimen of labor to earn the money required to live as the rich do. But do the "trinkets" his wealth affords him repay the labor he spent to get them?

To obtain the conveniencies which these afford, he submits in the first year, nay in the first month of his application, to more fatigue of body and more uneasiness of mind than he could have suffered through the whole of his life from the want of them. (TMS IV.i.8)

In Smith's parable, the son does not realize the mistake he made in his calculation until it is too late—not, that is, until:

in the last dregs of life, his body wasted with toil and diseases, his mind galled and ruffled by the memory of a thousand injuries and disappointments which he imagines he has met with from the injustice of his enemies, or from the perfidy and ingratitude of his friends, that he begins at last to find that wealth and greatness are mere trinkets of frivolous utility, no more adapted for procuring ease of body or tranquillity of mind than the tweezer-cases of the lover of toys; and like them too, more troublesome to the person who carries them about with him than all the advantages they can afford him are commodious. (TMS IV.i.8)

This is, to put it mildly, a rather cynical view of the activity of commercial society and the benefits of wealth, and not what one would expect from perhaps the "father" of commercial society. But the position is consistent with the view that happiness

consists in tranquility. If that is true, then activity, work, and
ambition, which are not conducive to tranquility, will upset one's
equipoise and endanger or defeat one's happiness.

Smith concludes his parable of the "poor man's son" with the
following: "And it is well that nature imposes upon us in this
manner. It is this deception which rouses and keeps in continual
motion the industry of mankind" (TMS IV.i.9). So Smith thinks
not only that we are naturally inclined to think our expenditure
of labor will pay off in the end (even if it usually does not), but
also that it is a good thing that we make this mistake—for this
"deception" provides the motivation that has led us to all the
industry and production that has made life so much better for
everyone.[4] This is another instance of a Smithian invisible-hand
argument. People intend only their own gain, and in its pursuit
they engage in activities that make everyone else better off as
well. But we also see in this passage, I believe, Smith feeling
pulled in two directions. On the one hand, if happiness consists
in tranquility, then to extend happiness we should not encourage people to labor in the service of delusional ambition. On
the other hand, when people do so labor, goods and services are
produced that improve everyone's material condition, making
all of our lives better. This captures one of the paradoxes of commercial life, which Smith perceives, right at the cusp of its
appearance in the world: the means for making our lives better
might not be the same as, and might even conflict with, the
means to making us happy.[5]

Justice versus Beneficence

In Chapter 3 we saw that Smith argues that the rules of "justice"
are often regarded as "sacred" and as the rules of the Deity Himself. I argued that this was not because the rules of justice are in
fact sacred or intended by God (though, of course, they might
be), but rather because observing them is so important to the
survival of any human society that they are universally discovered and taught and that their breach is universally punished.
The other rules of virtue—those that pertain to the many aspects
of beneficence—are, as Smith says, the

> ornament which embellishes, not the foundation which
> supports the building [that is human society], and which it

was, therefore, sufficient to recommend, but by no means necessary to impose. Justice, on the contrary, is the main pillar that upholds the whole edifice. If it is removed, the great, the immense fabric of human society, that fabric which to raise and support seems in this world, if I may say so, to have been the peculiar and darling care of Nature, must in a moment crumble into atoms. (TMS II.ii.3.4)

This means that the protection of justice is more important—indeed crucial—for any society, and no other virtue enjoys this level of importance.

Smith will argue that the state is therefore justified in enforcing justice. But it is not justified in enforcing the rules of beneficence. Why not? Smith says that injustice, unlike a failing in beneficence, constitutes the commission of "real positive evil" or "injury" instead of merely not having done a "good office." If I have acted unjustly I have taken "positive" action to do you an actual "evil" or "harm"; by contrast, if I failed to be beneficent to you, I took no positive action against you, but only refrained from taking positive action on your behalf. Writes Smith:

> Beneficence is always free, it cannot be extorted by force, the mere want of it exposes to no punishment; because the mere want of beneficence tends to do no real positive evil. It may disappoint of the good which might reasonably have been expected, and upon that account it may justly excite dislike and disapprobation: it cannot, however, provoke any resentment which mankind will go along with. (TMS II.ii.1.3)

Smith goes on to explain that whereas an impartial spectator would approve punishment, even by third parties, of breaches of justice, no such spectator would approve punishment of breaches of gratitude, charity, generosity, or friendship. Smith gives two reasons. First, the virtues of beneficence can be fulfilled only when freely acted upon; when we try to coerce them, we remove from them the essential element—namely free choice—that makes them virtues. "What friendship, what generosity, what charity, would prompt us to do with universal approbation, is still more free, and can still less be extorted by force than the duties of gratitude" (TMS II.ii.1.3).

The second reason Smith believes that only breaches of justice warrant punishment is connected to his conception of the nature of justice, in contradistinction to the nature of other virtues:

> The rules of justice may be compared to the rules of grammar; the rules of the other virtues, to the rules which critics lay down for the attainment of what is sublime and elegant in composition. The one, are precise, accurate, and indispensable. The other, are loose, vague, and indeterminate, and present us rather with a general idea of the perfection we ought to aim at, than afford us any certain and infallible directions for acquiring it. (TMS III.6.11)

Recall that Smith has argued that justice comprises just three central rules: respect one another's person, respect one another's property, and respect one another's voluntary contracts and agreements (see TMS II.ii.2.2). On the Smithian conception, justice is thus a "negative" virtue, meaning that it requires one merely to refrain from doing positive evil to others; as Smith says, in one of his most striking passages, "We may often fulfil all the rules of justice by sitting still and doing nothing" (TMS II. ii.1.10). Thus the rules of justice are, like the rules of grammar, few and clear, and their breaches are easily and (nearly) universally recognized. The rules of the other virtues, however, are by contrast many and ambiguous, and so dependent on particular circumstances that general rules of application are difficult to formulate. It is easy to know that one should not steal from another, and most instances of theft are readily recognizable by everyone. Yet how does one know whether I was sufficiently generous toward my colleagues today? Or sufficiently charitable toward my children? It may be that, like Justice Potter Stewart on "obscenity," we can recognize sufficient generosity or charity when we see it. But then we have to *see* it, in full knowledge of the relevant local details of a particular circumstance, to know whether proper beneficence obtained or not.

The distinction Smith draws between justice and all the other virtues he groups under the heading "beneficence"[6] has clear political implications for him. Because society "cannot subsist unless the laws of justice are tolerably observed" (TMS II.ii.3.6), society is therefore justified in enforcing the rules of justice: this becomes a, even the, central purpose of the state. But because (1) beneficence "is less essential to the existence of society than justice" (TMS II.ii.3.3), because (2) its absence is merely the absence of a positive good rather than the infliction of a positive evil, because (3) coerced beneficence is no virtue at all, and because (4) it is difficult to judge proper beneficence from afar: for all these reasons Smith argues that the judging and enforcement of proper beneficence should not fall within the state's purview. Thus the baseline for a Smithian state is quite limited: protections of person, property, and voluntary contract, punishments for attacks on person or property or breach of contract, and—little else. This is the limited government of what became known as "liberalism," so-called because it envisioned a stated limited to enforcing "negative" justice and leaving people otherwise free to direct their own lives.

It is important to note that Smith does not arrive at his recommendations about the limits of proper state authority by deducing them from a conception of natural law or natural human rights—as, for example, John Locke (1632–1704) does in his 1690 *Second Treatise of Government*, which also had profound effect on the founding of the United States.[7] Instead of relying on natural law, Smith bases his recommendations on our informed estimations of which social institutions give the best hope for human flourishing. Because Smith believes history shows that people do better under conditions of limited government, the strong presumption will be against third-party interposition into human affairs and in favor of allowing individuals to find their own ways. As Smith will articulate further in his WN, he thus recommends a largely—though not completely—laissez-faire state.

Although Smith's recommendations are consistent with those of many minimal-state theorists today, Smith, unlike many such proponents, endorses a liberalism that is pragmatic: he is willing to allow for exceptions to the default presumptions if there are specific cases in which local circumstances warrant it. For example, Smith allows that because a local

civil magistrate is entrusted with the power not only of preserving the public peace by restraining injustice, but of promoting the prosperity of the commonwealth, [. . .] he may prescribe rules, therefore, which not only prohibit mutual injuries among fellow-citizens, but command mutual good offices to a certain degree. (TMS II.ii.1.8)

Some commentators find a contradiction in Smith here, while
others find the seeds of a much later, "progressive" liberalism.[8]
I find neither. One must note, first, that Smith's language in
the passage is carefully crafted to indicate the rarity of such
exceptions. The magistrate "may" (not "must" or even "will")
prescribe such rules, Smith concedes, but he adds this robust
qualification:

> Of all the duties of a law-giver, however, this, perhaps, is that
> which it requires the greatest delicacy and reserve to execute
> with propriety and judgment. To neglect it altogether exposes
> the commonwealth to many gross disorders and shocking
> enormities, and to push it too far is destructive of all liberty,
> security, and justice. (TMS II.ii.1.8)

These are the words of a man of wide experience who understands that human affairs are complicated and that we often
overestimate our ability to excogitate moral or political principles that will hold for all times and all places. It is a simple but
profound insight that almost all principles have exceptions, but
those exceptions must be rare and specially defended. On the
other hand, he also recognizes that the dangers of tyranny are
real and must always be guarded against, even when our would-be
leaders do what they do in the name of our own good. Such a
position—which I would call "pragmatic liberalism"—may not
satisfy those who want inviolable or exceptionless principles, but
it is consistent with, and indeed flows from, Smith's belief that
although we can draw lessons from history we are not infallible
and those lessons are always subject to potential revision based
on further review.

Thus Smith's political theory is in an important sense
analogous to his moral theory. I argued in Chapter 3 that the
Smithian market-mechanism that gives rise to our moral rules
and judgments enjoy a "middle-way" objectivity: although they
are not derived from an immutable, transcendent order, neither
are they dependent on any single person's whim. They are facts
of our social existence, and they thus constitute a background
framework within which we must all operate. Although some
aspects of this framework may change over time, other aspects
are so important for the survival and success of our communities
that they will change only slowly if at all. Similarly, I now suggest,

with Smith's political principles. They derive neither from a transcendent conception of reason or natural law, nor from a religious conception of the soul or of human dignity. Instead, Smith sees them as determined by the results of numerous experiments people have run of different kinds of social arrangements throughout human history. The specific recommendations Smith makes of the scope and nature of proper government power are anchored by what he believes to be human nature and the facts of human existence; although some local exceptions might be specially justified, these recommendations are a presumptive default against which potential exceptions should be adjudged. Smith's position attempts to strike a balance between, on the one hand, respect for the "rule of law" (in this case, rules limiting government authority), and allowing some scope for human discretion, on the other. It is thus neither incoherent nor anticipatory of modern progressive liberalism. It is rather the liberalism that arguably informed, among others, the Founding Fathers of the United States of America. Here is Thomas Jefferson, for example, in his First Inaugural Address of 1801:

> a wise and frugal Government, which shall restrain men from injuring one another, shall leave them otherwise free to regulate their own pursuits of industry and improvement, and shall not take from the mouth of labor the bread it has earned. This is the sum of good government, and this is necessary to close the circle of our felicities.

Jefferson could have taken that right from Smith.

The "Man of System"

We now have before us the basic elements of the political economy Smith develops in TMS. Before turning to examine his more extensive and focused treatment in WN, let us look at another passage in TMS that bears on his position and dovetails with an extended argument Smith will make in WN. This is Smith's powerful discussion of the "man of system."

In the sixth part of TMS, Smith discusses "the character of virtue," exploring (1) how one's virtue affects one's own happiness, (2) how it affects others' happiness, and (3) the crucial importance of "self-command" in the virtuous life.[9] Because self-command is, Smith argues, indispensable in disciplining oneself to act in accordance with any virtue—to be generous or charitable or humane one must be first able to control one's behavior—Smith argues that self-command gives all the other virtues "their principal lustre" (TMS VI.iii.11), and he dedicates many pages to exploring its importance.[10] In Smith's investigation of the second point—how one's virtue affects others' happiness—Smith has a brief but potent discussion of how individuals can affect others' prospects in either positive or negative ways. In this context Smith raises the topic of the love of one's country, and he distinguishes between two principles of patriotism: "first, a certain respect and reverence for that constitution or form of government which is actually established; and secondly, an earnest desire to render the condition of our fellow-citizens as safe, respectable, and happy as we can" (TMS VI.ii.2.11). As Smith says, in times of peace these two principles usually "coincide and lead to the same conduct" (TMS VI.ii.2.12); in times of turmoil, however, factions can arise that can inflame people to "madness" or "fanaticism" (TMS VI.ii.2.15).

In the latter times, those of turmoil, Smith writes that there are two different kinds of leaders who may arise. The first is a kind of pragmatic conservative:

> The man whose public spirit is prompted altogether by humanity and benevolence, will respect the established powers and privileges even of individuals, and still more those of the great orders and societies, into which the state is divided. Though he should consider some of them as in some measure abusive, he will content himself with moderating, what he often cannot annihilate without great violence. [. . .] He will accommodate, as well as he can, his public arrangements to the confirmed habits and prejudices of the people; [. . . and] like Solon, when he cannot establish the best system of laws, he will endeavour to establish the best that the people can bear. (TMS VI.ii.2.16)

If this description reminds the reader of the conservatism of Edmund Burke, that is no coincidence: Burke was an admiring reader of Smith.[11] Smith describes a second kind of leader in such circumstances, however, and this one is no Burkean:

The man of system, on the contrary, is apt to be very wise in his own conceit; and is often so enamoured with the supposed beauty of his own ideal plan of government, that he cannot suffer the smallest deviation from any part of it. He goes on to establish it completely and in all its parts, without any regard either to the great interests, or to the strong prejudices which may oppose it. He seems to imagine that he can arrange the different members of a great society with as much ease as the hand arranges the different pieces upon a chess-board. He does not consider that the pieces upon the chess-board have no other principle of motion besides that which the hand impresses upon them; but that, in the great chess-board of human society, every single piece has a principle of motion of its own, altogether different from that which the legislature might chuse to impress upon it. (TMS VI.ii.2.17)

This leader—who sounds rather more like the French Revolution's Robespierre (1758–94), a principal of the Great Terror and the object of much of Burke's invective—embodies for Smith many common, and dangerous, errors of statesmen. Smith continues with a damning indictment of such political leaders:

But to insist upon establishing, and upon establishing all at once, and in spite of all opposition, every thing which [the man of system's] idea may seem to require, must often be the highest degree of arrogance. It is to erect his own judgment into the supreme standard of right and wrong. It is to fancy himself the only the only wise and worthy man in the commonwealth, and that his fellow-citizens should accommodate themselves to him and not he to them. [. . . Such people] consider the state as made for themselves, not themselves for the state. (TMS VI.ii.2.18)

The dangers of the "man of system" will become a recurring theme in Smith's WN. As we shall see, in WN Smith again and again warns of our tendency to overestimate our ability to know what is good or right for others, of our willingness to substitute our judgment for others, coercively if necessary, and of our willingness to punish citizens who fail, as they inevitably will, to hew perfectly to our "ideal plan of government." We turn next to explore the political economy Smith develops in WN, but here I wish to suggest that Smith's discussion of the "man of system" coheres with the rest of TMS's political economy, and indeed puts an exclamation point on it. Not only is the presumption in favor of limited state authority, but we must be ever wary of those who wish to expand state authority—and thus restrict individual liberty—in the name of their bold and beautiful plan for making our lives better.

Notes

[1] This "early draft" was discovered by W. R. Scott and first published in 1937. It is reprinted in the Appendix to LJ, 562–81.

[2] A recent study of "political economy" in Smith and his contemporaries is Aspromourgos (2009). See also Teichgraeber (1986).

[3] This is apparently in addition to the loving relationships also required for happiness, as discussed in Chapter 4.

[4] See Schliesser (2002).

[5] The question is whether we can have the former while still maintaining the latter. I think the answer is yes, but it requires a shift in the nature of our search for happiness. I develop this argument in Otteson (2010b). See also Hanley (2009).

[6] I note that Smith is careful not to confuse *beneficence* and *benevolence*. The latter, meaning merely *wishing* someone well, does not concern Smith here; he is concerned, rather, with the former, which means actually *doing* someone well. Later in TMS Smith explains why he thinks we are, properly, more concerned with people's actions than with their mere sentiments; see TMS III.iii.3.

[7] For a discussion of Smith's affect on the founding of America, see Adair (1998) and Fleischacker (2002).

[8] For discussion, along with the claim that Smith contradicts himself, see Fleischacker (2005), chapter 8.

[9] For an excellent discussion of the important of part six to the rest of TMS, see Hanley (2009), esp. chapter 3.

[10] At almost 30 pages, the section entitled "Of Self-command" (VI.iii) is one of the longest in TMS.

[11] See, for example, letters 38, 145, 230, 263, and 265 in C.

Chapter 6

Political Economy in *The Wealth of Nations*

Judged by its influence, Adam Smith's *Inquiry into the Nature and Causes of the Wealth of Nations* (WN) must be considered one of the most important works of the second millennium. As with any great work that stands at the forefront of an entire discipline, Smith's WN has its share of mistakes; and of course it is not entirely original, building and drawing, as it does, on the work of many others.[1] In Chapter 8, I survey some of the "misses" of WN. But this chapter has a different goal, one that can be illustrated by analogy to Aristotle. If one wanted to know what the discipline of, say, physics currently holds, reading Aristotle would not help; similarly, if one were to read Aristotle to judge what he says against the current state of thought in any of various scientific disciplines of which Aristotle is one of the progenitors, one would generate a rather long and tedious list of Aristotelian errors. On the other hand, if one is interested to know how one of the greatest of human minds wrestled with enduring questions of the human condition, then one could profitably begin with Aristotle; and Aristotle's penetrating reflections on scientific method—not his roster of scientific facts—are deeply instructive as well. I submit Smith stands in a similar position. WN is a profound and extended meditation on human nature and on the nature of certain kinds of human social relations. It extends the theoretical "market model" Smith developed in *The Theory of Moral Sentiments* (TMS) and applies it, with startling results, to a large but specific area of human sociality, namely what we now think of as "economics." And it makes a powerful yet intuitive case for a range of claims that have become the mainstays of modern economic thought.

For all these reasons WN warrants serious study and repays extended examination. We can, unfortunately, look at only some of the highlights. Thus before proceeding I issue the disclaimer once again that we must pass over in silence much of value in the work, and I again recommend that the reader wanting a truer understanding of Smith's WN should read the great work itself.

Here, then, are the topics we shall address in this chapter: (1) Smith's treatment of the division of labor; (2) the conception of human nature that informs his examination; (3) his series of arguments that culminate in the famous "invisible hand" passage; (4) the proper scope and purposes of the Smithian state; and finally (5), Smith's theory of property. In the next chapter we discuss the connecting principles that link the analysis in TMS with the analysis in WN.

The Division of Labor

It might surprise the reader of WN to discover that Smith does not locate the key to wealth in natural resources, in favorable climate, or in the alleged superiority of one race of human beings over another. Each of these suggestions was advanced by various people in Smith's day, so they were ready to hand. Instead, however, Smith focuses on the division of labor and, in particular, the human ingenuity to which it gives release.

"The greatest improvement in the productive powers of labour," Smith writes, "and the greater part of the skill, dexterity, and judgment with which it is any where directed, or applied, seem to have been the effects of the division of labour" (WN I.i.1). To illustrate the claim Smith gives a now famous example of a pin factory. A single person, according to Smith, could, working on his own, "with his utmost industry, make one pin in a day, and certainly could not make twenty" (WN I.i.3). By contrast, when the labor of making a pin is divided among ten people each of whom focuses on a small range of the operations required to make a pin, Smith writes: "Those ten persons, therefore, could make among them upwards of forty-eight thousand pins in a day" (ibid.). That means that each person's share is 4,800 pins per day—a 240-fold increase over what each could do on his own! Now perhaps Smith exaggerates. Assume he is off by 50 percent; assume, even, that he is off by 90 percent. The production from an efficient division of labor would still constitute an astonishing increase over an undivided operation.

What explains this increase? Smith attributes it to three causes:

first, to the increase of dexterity in every particular workman; secondly, to the saving of the time which is commonly lost in passing from one species of work to another; and lastly, to the invention of a great number of machines which facilitate and abridge labour, and enable one man to do the work of many. (WN I.i.5)

These three circumstances, Smith argues, enable the combined production of a number of workers to far outstrip the production of all of them added together when working in isolation. It may have taken Henry Ford, over a century later, to understand how to fully exploit this idea, but it was Smith who locates the beginnings of the spectacular increases in wealth since the eighteenth century in this simple but profound observation.

Although the example of the pin factory provides a dramatic illustration of the principle, Smith argues that "In every other art and manufacture, the effects of the division of labour are similar to what they are in this very trifling one" (WN I.i.4). So here are the steps of his generalized argument:

1. Division of labor allows an increase in production.
2. An increase in production leads, other things being equal, to greater availability and thus a decrease in price.
3. Greater availability and decreasing prices enable more people to purchase and enjoy the good in question.
4. As this process is repeated across industries, more and more people can enjoy more and more goods.
5. Thus increasing division of labor leads to greater overall prosperity.

Smith's own summary of his argument:

It is the great multiplication of the productions of all the different arts, in consequence of the division of labour, which occasions, in a well-governed society, that universal opulence which extends itself to the lowest ranks of the people. Every workman has a great quantity of his own work to dispose of beyond what he himself has occasion for; and every other workman being exactly in the same situation, he is enabled to exchange a great quantity of his own goods for a great quantity, or, what comes to the same thing, for the price of a great quantity of theirs. He supplies them abundantly with what they have occasion for, and they accommodate him as amply with what he has occasion for, and a general plenty diffuses itself through all the different ranks of the society. (WN I.i.10)

Smith's argument is elegantly simple, but it contains many assumptions and implications that Smith will develop later in the work. Note, for example, Smith's use of the terms "universal opulence" and "general plenty": these indicate not only that Smith is genuinely concerned with the welfare of the least among us, but also that one of the principal reasons Smith will come to endorse a market-based commercial society is its beneficial effects on the poor. Smith's argument here is founded upon a concern for allowing people to lead better lives as they themselves understand them, and when one lives in a society, as Smith did, in which some people are so desperately poor that they might not eat again today, the first goal must be to increase the total amount of basic goods available for consumption.

Note also the high degree of interdependence that the benefits of division of labor imply. As each of us enjoys the "general plenty" enabled by division of labor, all members of society become more closely united by trade and commerce. We give up the older model of small groups of independent but poor people who procure or make everything they have all on their own, for a new model in which people contribute only a fraction of the total labor involved in producing goods but enjoy many more of them. Smith sees this as a tremendously beneficial tradeoff. He describes in positively glowing terms how even a "coarse and rough" "woollen coat" that "covers the day-labourer" "is the produce of the joint labour of a great multitude of workmen"; Smith continues: "The shepherd, the sorter of the wool, the wool-comber or carder, the dyer, the scribbler, the spinner, the weaver, the fuller, the dresser, with many others, must all join their different arts in order to complete even this homely production" (WN I.i.11). After going on to list many more people and occupations involved directly or indirectly in the production of the workman's woolen coat, Smith draws this conclusion:

if we examine, as I say, all these things, and consider what a variety of labour is employed about each of them, we shall be sensible that without the assistance and co-operation of many thousands, the very meanest person in a civilized country could not be provided, even according to, what we very falsely imagine, the easy and simple manner in which he is commonly accommodated. (ibid.)

This is clearly a celebration for Smith. The manifold interdependence of each person on each other in a "civilized" commercial society not only unites us one to another, but it provides us with far more of the things we want than any of us could have had on his own. By contrast, Jean-Jacques Rousseau (1712–78), to name one prominent example, was not pleased with the changes commercial society brings. Interdependence, Rousseau argued, was not freedom at all because it was still dependence, and therefore a kind of slavery. According to Rousseau, to whatever degree one was unable to provide for one's desires entirely upon one's own, to that same degree one's independence, and thus one's humanity, was compromised.[2] So whereas Smith sees commercial society as freeing us, especially the least of us, from the rigors of a parsimonious nature, enabling ever more of us to better our condition, Rousseau sees it as enslaving us, rendering us weak and dependent, no longer the robust, though solitary, creatures he imagines we should be and perhaps once were.[3] It turns out that Smith will articulate later in WN his own concerns about some damaging effects that extensive division of labor might have on workers; we turn to Smith's concerns, which are not unrelated to Rousseau's, later in this chapter. But for now, and in this initial discussion in the first few pages of WN, Smith presents the division of labor as an enormous benefit for any society lucky enough to enjoy it.

Note one other important point in the earlier passage from Smith: the implication, contained in Smith's discussion of what each of us "has occasion for," that people have varied tastes and preferences and that Smith will refrain from judgment about whose tastes are better than others, which are legitimate and which not, and so on. One central argument Smith will make in WN is that third parties are typically incompetent to determine for others what the best uses of their resources are. Smith's claim is not that there are not in fact better or worse choices a person might make. Rather, his concern arises from the question of who is in the best position to judge for an individual what the best uses of his resources are. Smith will answer that legislators, statesmen, or other distant third parties are typically not in good positions to make these determinations. On the contrary, typically the person best positioned to make such decisions is the individual in question himself.

When Smith claims that it is the widespread existence of the division of labor in a society that distinguishes it as "civilized" instead of "savage,"[4] it is not merely because of the greater wealth of the former as compared to that of the latter. It is also because in a commercial society "the most dissimilar geniuses are of use to one another," and thus people with widely varying talents, skills, and interests can find a place and home (WN I.ii.5). Suppose you are the sort of person who enjoys, and has a talent for, translating ancient texts; or suppose you like to write music or novels or poetry; or suppose you are good at observing, categorizing, and speculating about the relations among different varieties of finches. In any of these circumstances, if your community does not have an extensive division of labor—which, as Smith points out, requires markets for trade and exchange—you may well just be out of luck. Among the "savage" hunting tribes, there is a very small range of activities that you will be required, or allowed, to do, and if your talents or interests point in different directions, woe to you. By contrast, Smith argues, in a commercial society, you will find many more opportunities than you otherwise would, many more niches that your peculiar talents and interests might serve and where they might thus not only be allowed but even encouraged and rewarded.

To give Rousseau his due, we might point out that, because people in a commercial society are dependent on others' taking an interest in their goods or services, there remains a danger that there will be no market for the activity you would like to pursue—in which case you will still have to settle for something other than what you ideally wanted. But that is always the case in a world of scarce resources, which would include any that Rousseau could inhabit. The available options are thus not either (1) satisfying everyone's desires or (2) satisfying no one's, but, rather, choosing a set of institutions that allow for relatively more people to satisfy relatively more of their desires. That is what Smith believes the commercial society offers, and the enlarged range of possibilities it opens up for people of all ranks in society is precisely what makes it, for Smith, "civilized." Instead of killing or ostracizing people with peculiar talents, as the "savage" societies do, the commercial society gives them the opportunity to give their talents a voice. What could be more civilized than that?

Human Nature

One recurring criticism of "capitalism" is the inequality it seems to entail: some inevitably have more than others, which some deem objectionable, even if everyone is better off overall.[5] There is an irony to this criticism, because Smith himself was deeply concerned with equality, and in particular with improving the prospects of the least among us. But the kind of equality Smith advocates is not an equality of material resources. He is interested to help the poorest lift themselves out of poverty, and his argument is that institutions encouraging division of labor, markets, and capital accumulation stand the best chance of doing so. In the course of developing this argument, Smith makes a radical claim: all human beings—regardless of race, nationality, or creed—are roughly equal in natural ability. "The difference," Smith says, "between the most dissimilar characters, between a philosopher and a common street porter, for example, seems to arise not so much from nature, as from habit, custom, and education" (WN I.ii.4). The equality of which Smith speaks, and which he assumes in his analysis, takes primarily three forms: first, we all have a natural, and uniquely human, "disposition to truck, barter, and exchange" (ibid.); second, we all wish to improve our material condition; and third, we are all motivated by self-interest, even when other motivations are present as well. Take each of these by turn.

First, as Smith emphasizes, other animals do not have a capacity for, and therefore do not engage in, exchange: "Nobody ever saw a dog make a fair and deliberate exchange of one bone for another with another dog" (WN I.ii.2). But humans of all stripes do, and this fact makes all humans more closely equal than different species of dog are to one another—or than any given human being is to any other animal (WN I.ii.5). Smith suggests that our natural propensity to truck, barter, and exchange might be a consequence of the natural human capacities of reason and speech, though he also allows that it might be an "original principle" in human nature (WN I.ii.2). Either way, it is present among all human societies, thus providing an important link among all humans.

Human beings of all times and places are also united, Smith believes, by their universal and constant desire to better their conditions. Smith writes:

> But the principle which prompts to save, is the desire of bettering our condition, a desire which, though generally calm and dispassionate, comes with us from the womb, and never leaves us till we go into the grave. In the whole interval which separates those two moments, there is scarce perhaps a single instant in which any man is so perfectly and completely satisfied with his situation, as to be without any wish of alteration or improvement, of any kind. (WN II.iii.28)

Smith repeats this claim several times in WN; here is one further example, which Smith couples with a criticism of government meddling in the market:

> The uniform, constant, and uninterrupted effort of every man to better his condition, the principle from which publick and national, as well as private opulence is originally derived, is frequently powerful enough to maintain the natural progress of things toward improvement, in spite both of the extravagance of government, and of the greatest errors of administration. (WN II.iii.31)

Smith takes this to be a basic fact of human nature, and it is a fundamental assumption both of his analysis of the nature and causes of wealth and of the recommendations he will make about the proper role and scope of government authority. It is, moreover, another link in the chain that binds all human beings to one another. Not only do we all wish to better our conditions—however each of us understands "bettering" them[6]—but doing so requires division of labor and markets that entail an extensive mutual dependence and cooperation.

Finally, all human beings, Smith thinks, are motivated by self-interest. By this Smith does not mean selfishness. His argument that we all wish to better our conditions assumes that we are often made better off when those we love or care about are made better off. So it is an expanded notion of "self-interest," including the interests of people who are important to us. Nor is Smith arguing that we feel no motivation aside from self-interest: only that it is probably always present, and thus that it—unlike, say, benevolence—can always, or nearly always, be relied upon. It is this claim one finds in the second-most-famous passage from WN:

> It is not from the benevolence of the butcher, the brewer, or the baker, that we expect our dinner, but from their regard to their own interest. We address ourselves, not to their humanity but to their self-love, and never talk to them of our own necessities but of their advantages. (WN I.ii.2)

Note that in this passage Smith is not arguing that people do not feel benevolence or that benevolence is never an appropriate motive—two misinterpretations on the basis of which one might mount obvious criticisms. Instead, Smith's argument comprehends two claims. First, in commercial relations—that is, when we are exchanging goods or services with one another—the routine or usual way of proceeding is by attempting to complete the exchange by making an offer we hope will satisfy the preferences of the other party to the exchange more than his current situation does. I desire the hot dog from the vender more than I do the $5 in my wallet, so I am willing to exchange one for the other; the vender has the opposite preferences, so we make a voluntary exchange that leaves us both better off. The overwhelming majority of market-based or commercial exchanges proceed in a similar way, making both parties (or all parties) simultaneously better off. This is why voluntary market exchanges are generally so beneficial: everyone wins.

The other claim Smith is making in this passage is a prediction: We are more likely to achieve a successful exchange if we appeal to our potential trading partner's "self-love." Again Smith is not claiming that people are moved only by self-love. His claim rests rather on his belief that one constant motivation of human action is self-interest, and further that one of the principal—though again not the only—reasons people engage in commercial activity is to gain the means to "better their condition." They want to make their lives better, as well as the lives of their family and friends and others they care about, and commercial activity helps provide them the means to do so. People have real, if limited, benevolence, and Smith's argument is not inconsistent with the claim that actors in markets can be motivated by motives like helping out their fellow men, serving their country, and so on. His argument instead is that you are more likely to have success in markets if you first seek to find ways to satisfy *others'* interests, and by so doing can you satisfy your own.

This conception of the relation among human beings in a commercial society gives a further indication of the reason Smith might think that commerce can be a "civilizing" force. The way one becomes successful in a commercial society is by finding ways to satisfy others' interests in the hopes of thereby satisfying one's own; one improves one's own condition by improving the condition and satisfying the interests of others. In a commercial society there is virtually no other way to succeed. Hence while a commercial society entails competition among people trying to succeed, and competition can produce stress or anxiety (not to mention winners and losers); nevertheless this competition results in the improvement of everyone's lot. This indeed is the genius of the Smithian commercial society: without requiring people to "love their neighbor" but only to act on their self-love, its mechanism channels this self-love to the mutual improvement of everyone. If Smith is right that self-interest is an abiding feature of humanity—and he would seem to have a point—then the challenge to the political economist is not to try to eliminate it but rather to devise institutions that direct it toward good ends, regardless of, even perhaps despite, people's own conscious intentions. This is precisely what Smith believes the commercial society does, and its relative success at turning men's minds away from mutual suspicion and bellicose antagonism to mutual exchange and trade he regards as a formidable civilizing force, and thus one tremendously beneficial, if unintentional, effect of commerce.

We can conclude our discussion of Smith's conception of human nature by relating the benefits he believes commercial society has to the claim we mentioned at the outset of this section about Smith's position on human equality. In an age in which the consensus held that humans were sharply divided along racial or class lines, with differences among the races or classes often held to reflect qualitative natural differences, Smith's claims that all humans are in fact roughly equal by nature, that their differences are due more to training than to nature, and that those trained differences are nevertheless rather trivial constitute a startling departure.[7] Smith's position in fact has two further radical implications: one, the analysis of commercial society and the nature and causes of wealth holds for all people, not merely for eighteenth-century Britons; two, a commercial society would benefit poor people anywhere in the world, and is thus to be recommended for everyone. In this way Smith saw himself fulfilling the Newtonian imperative of discovering universal laws describing the regular behavior of all the entities—in Smith's case, human beings—under examination. But I believe he also took enormous delight, and indeed relief, in what he took to be the discovery of those institutions that would allow *all* humans to continue to better their condition. For Smith, then, the investigation into political economy, and the promulgation of its discoveries, was a profoundly moral undertaking, and his hopes about its prospects of alleviating the suffering of the poor drove him to dedicate decades of is life to its study.

The Invisible Hand and the Great Mind Fallacy

The claim that commercial activity can lead to unintended benefits brings us to Smith's most famous argument, his "invisible hand" argument. Smith's argument actually comprises three separate arguments—the Local Knowledge Argument, the Economizer Argument, and the Invisible Hand Argument—and it implicates an important, and recurring, intellectual mistake that I will call the Great Mind Fallacy (GMF).[8]

One of the passages we discussed in Chapter 5 is Smith's discussion of the "man of system," in which he criticizes the legislator who believes he can arrange human beings "with as much ease as the hand arranges the different pieces upon a chess-board" (TMS VI.ii.2.17). The "man of system," according to Smith, understands that

the pieces upon the chess-board have no other principle of motion besides that which the hand impresses upon them; but [he fails to realize] that, in the great chess-board of human society, every single piece has a principle of motion of its own, altogether different from that which the legislature might chuse to impress upon it. (TMS VI.ii.2.18)

Because human beings have their own ideas, a legislator wishing for them to conform to his comprehensive plan, however beautiful and attractive in itself, is bound to be frustrated. Human beings upset patterns, as philosopher Robert Nozick said,[9] and they do so in numerous and unpredictable ways. Hence, Smith argues, the legislator is faced with either giving up on his beautiful plan or attempting to impose it by force.

Smith builds his position on the basis of three central arguments. First is his *Local Knowledge Argument:* because everyone has unique knowledge of his own "local" situation, including his goals, his desires, and the opportunities available to him, each individual is therefore the person best positioned to make decisions about what courses of action he should take to achieve his goals.

> What is the species of domestick industry which his capital can employ, and of which the produce is likely to be of the greatest value, every individual, it is evident, can, in his local situation, judge much better than any statesman or lawgiver can do for him. (WN IV.ii.10)[10]

That does not mean that people are infallible in judging their own situations; rather, it means that their unique local knowledge provides them a better chance of knowing how best to use their resources and what courses of actions to take to achieve their goals. The further away a decision-maker is from the person those decisions affect, the less likely it is that the decisions will be good ones. Thus distant legislators are quite ill-positioned.

Second is Smith's *Economizer Argument*, which holds that because each of us continuously seeks to better his own condition, each of us seeks out efficient uses of his resources and labor, given his peculiar and unique circumstances, to maximize their productive output and return on his investment.

> The uniform, constant, and uninterrupted effort of every man to better his condition, the principle from which publick and national, as well as private opulence is originally derived, is frequently powerful enough to maintain the natural progress of things toward improvement, in spite both of the extravagance of government, and of the greatest errors of administration. (WN II.iii.31)[11]

Finally, third, is Smith's famous *Invisible Hand Argument*, which holds that as each of us strives to better his own condition, as provided for in the Economizer Argument, by exploiting his unique reservoirs of knowledge, as provided for in the Local Knowledge Argument, each of us thereby simultaneously, though unintentionally, betters the condition of others. This argument is trickier than it seems, so some delicacy is required to capture it.[12] Here is Smith's phrasing of this argument:

> As every individual, therefore, endeavours as much as he can . . . to direct [his] industry that its produce may be of the greatest value; every individual necessarily labours to render the annual revenue of the society as great as he can. He generally, indeed, neither intends to promote the public interest, nor knows how much he is promoting it. . . . [H]e intends only his own security; and by directing that industry in such a manner as its produce may be of the greatest value, he intends only his own gain, and he is in this, as in many other cases, led by an invisible hand to promote an end which was no part of his intention. (WN IV.ii.9)[13]

Smith's claim is not that people do not act intentionally, but rather that they typically act with only their own, local purposes in mind, unconcerned with, even unaware of, whatever larger effects their behavior has on unknown others. Now their "local" purposes are not necessarily related only to themselves, since Smith believes they include concerns about family and friends as well. Our concern for others fades, Smith thinks, the farther away from us they are, but he thinks our concern for others closer to ourselves is real and undeniable. So we act in attempts to satisfy our own purposes, whatever they are, but because we are "economizers" we tend to try to expend the least amount of our own energy possible while at the same time trying to get the largest, richest, or most extensive achievement of our goals as possible. We seek, as it were, the best possible return on our investment of our energies.

According to the Invisible Hand Argument, this search for efficient use of our energies happily benefits not only ourselves and those close to us (the direct objects of our concern), but it also benefits others, even others totally unknown to us. As we have seen, this happens because when we specialize or concentrate our efforts on some small range of tasks or talents, we usually produce more than we can ourselves consume or use, which means we create a surplus that we can trade or sell away; that, in turn, means that the overall stock of goods and services increases, and their prices thus decrease, for everyone. Additionally, as we seek out exchanges, forms of contract and trade, and so on that serve our local interests, others may learn from us and imitate our successes and avoid our failures, thereby saving themselves time and energy, thereby enabling them to go marginally further than we did in securing their—and thus, indirectly, everyone else's—ends. According to Smith, then, the "invisible hand" effects a "general plenty," a "universal opulence which extends itself to the lowest ranks of the people" (WN I.i.10). The wealth does not stay only in the hands of the person generating it or only in the hands of the already wealthy, Smith argues, but spreads to and is enjoyed by all (if not to the same extent).

Pulling Smith's three arguments together now, what Smith describes as "the obvious and simple system of natural liberty" (WN IV.ix.51) is a society-wide allowance of the invisible-hand mechanism to operate. Here is how he concludes the argument:

> All systems either of preference or of restraint, therefore, being thus completely taken away, the obvious and simple system of natural liberty establishes itself of its own accord. Every man, as long as he does not violate the laws of justice, is left perfectly free to pursue his own interest his own way, and to bring both his industry and capital into competition with those of any other man, or order of men. The sovereign is completely discharged from a duty, in the attempting to perform which he must always be exposed to innumerable delusions, and for the proper performance of which no human wisdom or knowledge could ever be sufficient; the duty of superintending the industry of private people, and of directing it towards the employments most suitable to the interest of the society. (WN IV.ix.51)[14]

I suggest that the Local Knowledge Argument, the Economizer Argument, and the Invisible Hand Argument form a comprehensive basis for Smith's political economy. Moreover, what

I propose to call Smith's Great Mind Fallacy builds on these three and puts the exclamation point on the argument. The GMF is summarized by Smith in two key passages. First is his "man of system" passage in TMS, which we have already discussed. The second comes in WN, directly after the "invisible hand" passage:

> The statesman, who should attempt to direct private people in what manner they ought to employ their capitals, would not only load himself with a most unnecessary attention, but assume an authority which could safely be trusted, not only to no single person, but to no council or senate whatever, and which would nowhere be so dangerous as in the hands of a man who had folly and presumption enough to fancy himself fit to exercise it. (WN IV.ii.10)

The statesman's attention is "unnecessary" because, according to the Local Knowledge, Economizer, and Invisible Hand arguments, people's decentralized and uncoordinated strivings to better their conditions are more likely to succeed than centralized and coordinated attempts would be; thus what the statesman would (or should) wish to achieve—bettering people's conditions—is more likely to happen if he does little beyond establishing a "tolerable administration of justice" (EPS IV.25). The "folly and presumption" of the statesman is manifested in his assumption that he can gather and process all the relevant information—what we might call the "knowledge problem."[15] And such a mistaken belief is "dangerous" because, Smith suggests, it inevitably leads the statesman to impose, or attempt to impose, his own plan for society—which Smith believes will almost inevitably be inferior to a decentralized and spontaneously created order.

Smith's argument holds that people commit the GMF when they believe that they themselves can overcome the knowledge problem, when they make political recommendations that presume that they can overcome them, or when they make recommendations that require someone else—legislators, regulators, the president, etc.—to have the ability to overcome these problems. The GMF is the belief, or hope, that there is someone out there smart enough and benevolent enough to make these decisions for us, leaving us peacefully secure in the knowledge that somebody somewhere is protecting and taking care of us.

It would be nice. Alas, here on earth there is no such Great Mind. And no fallible human beings—not even "government experts"—ever will be.

What Smith's Political Economy Rules Out

Smith's chain of arguments culminating in the GMF suggests, in two principal and connected ways, that we should limit the scope of the state's authority over individuals' decisions about how best to employ their capitals. First, the Local Knowledge Argument implies that third parties will not have the knowledge required to make competent decisions about how other individuals should behave in order to achieve their (the individuals') goals and ends. Second, the Economizer Argument and the Invisible Hand Argument imply that granting individuals wide scope, within the rules of (negative) justice,[16] to pursue their own ends will tend to benefit not only themselves but everyone else as well.

The scope of facts that legislators allegedly cannot know about their citizens is not trivial, for it comprises the values, circumstances, and estimations necessary for selecting courses of action appropriate to individuals' ends. Without this knowledge, one is engaging in speculation that, according to the GMF, presumes a competence that theorists, legislators, and regulators do not possess. Smith's argument thus presents a serious challenge to contemporary political philosophy, much of which contains careful delineations of the decisions that third parties are presumed competent to make and the areas of human life government is presumed competent to superintend. Perhaps it would help illustrate Smith's political economy if we contrasted the potential legislative activities his arguments rule out with examples of what some contemporary philosophers wish to rule in.

Here is what law professor Cass Sunstein believes that legislators or regulators should make decisions about or provide for citizens: "liberal education" and "the inculcation of critical and disparate attitudes toward prevailing conceptions of the good"; "aggressive initiatives with respect to the arts and broadcasting" including "subsidizing public broadcasting, ensuring a range of disparate programming, or calling for high-quality programming"; investigating and educating people about the correct "risks of hazardous activity"; and not only enforcing nondiscrimination policies but also investigating and educating people regarding "the beliefs of both beneficiaries and victims of existing injustice [that] are affected by dissonance-reducing strategies," such as "blaming the victim."[17] Sunstein argues that "democratic controls" over people's preferences are required to "protect people either from unjust background conditions or a sheer lack of options"; these controls will entail the need to provide information, for which "governmentally required disclosure of risks in the workplace is a highly laudable strategy." He continues:

> In a few cases, however, these milder initiatives are inadequate, and other measures are necessary. A moderately intrusive strategy could involve economic incentives, which might take the form of tax advantages or cash payments. For example, the government might give financial inducements to day-care centers as a way of relieving child-care burdens. Such a system might well be preferable to direct transfers of money to families, a policy that will predictably lead many more women to stay at home. In view of the sources of and consequences of the differential distribution of child-care burdens, it is fully legitimate for the government to take steps in the direction of equalization. (1997: 28)

To forestall the likely objection that his paternalism is antiliberal, Sunstein claims that "liberalism does not forbid citizens [. . .] from enacting their considered judgments into law, or from counteracting, through the provision of opportunities and information, preferences and beliefs that have adjusted to an unjust status quo."[18]

More recently, Sunstein has argued in his book *Nudge*, co-authored with economist Richard H. Thaler, that the government should pursue a course of "libertarian paternalism."[19] According to Thaler and Sunstein, libertarian paternalism endorses framing the presentation of options, arranging incentives, and deliberately creating psychological impressions that encourage people to make good decisions (the paternalistic part), while still allowing them the freedom to choose otherwise (the libertarian part). Their book discusses the various ways that people can be encouraged—"nudged"—to make decisions that planners believe are good ones, or at least relatively better ones, without overtly coercing people and indeed often without people realizing they were nudged in the first place. Examples they cite are the deliberate arrangement of foods in a cafeteria to increase the amount of fruits and vegetables people select, the purposefully designed default settings in investment and retirement plans to increase rates of certain kinds of investment by automatically enrolling one unless one deliberately opts out, and the reframing of discussions of teen drinking and smoking to create the impression that only fringe minorities engage in those unhealthful activities.[20] Thaler and Sunstein emphasize the importance of allowing free choice, and the examples just cited seem fairly pedestrian by today's standards. But their wish to avoid the vices of "hard-line" antipaternalists and "ardent" libertarians (ibid., 236 and 242, respectively) leads them to recommend nudging people in further ways that reflect what they believe is the general consensus or expert opinion about what is good for people. These include occasions on which people "need a good nudge for choices that have delayed effects; those that are difficult, infrequent, and offer poor feedback; and those for which the relation between choice and experience is ambiguous" (ibid., 76–7). An example they claim fits these qualifications is reduction of our energy use, which they argue is one "socially desirable behavior" among many that might call for governmental nudges.[21] Their goal, they say, is not to rob people of their freedom to choose, but rather to help individuals make choices that the individuals themselves *would* have made *if* these individuals "had paid full attention and possessed complete information, unlimited cognitive abilities, and complete self-control" (ibid., 5).

The Sunstein and Thaler argument runs afoul of the Smithian GMF in a handful of related ways. First, although it might be possible to determine what decisions the majority of people would make in many cases, it is far more difficult—perhaps impossible—to determine what would be best, or even relatively better, in any individual cases. Second, because they argue that appropriate nudges should inform regulatory policy and even legislation,[22] their argument apparently presumes a relatively fixed and static state of affairs in the world: a fixed set of people and goals and obstacles to overcome, and thus a relatively fixed set of potential solutions to those obstacles and means to achieve their goals that can be captured in regulatory policy and law. The Smithian conception of the world, however, is one that is dynamic and changing, at least at the margins. People's goals, and their available means to achieve those goals, are frequently changing, and they will be facing new, and new kinds, of obstacles to achieving them. Third parties cannot anticipate these changes (even first parties have difficulty doing so), and hence many "nudges" that seem appropriate now might be obsolete and even counter-productive in a short while—and yet will remain fixed in law or regulation. Third, note that their suggested areas of nudgings—wherever choices have delayed effects, are difficult and infrequent, and so on—are quite broad, indeed without clear limits ex ante.[23]

Many other thinkers face similar problems.[24] Working out the range of information required to implement their extensive lists of putative state duties or responsibilities reveals the presumption of an impressive, and surprisingly large, body of knowledge. The issue is not simply that life involves tradeoffs and that the state must often make difficult choices—though that is of course true. Instead, the Smithian argument is that it is a mistake to presume that third parties can possess the information necessary to make these determinations. Nor is the claim that there are no correct answers to these questions or that all answers are equally good; rather, the large number of individual variations in each of the large number of situations in which people find themselves generate multiple options and variables, and thus the decisions the legislator must make quickly become inordinately complicated. The presumption that these equations can be solved centrally is the "conceit" of Smith's "man of system," and to believe it is to commit the GMF.

Is the GMF a Fallacy?

One might argue that the GMF is not a true fallacy after all. One might claim, for example, that the experts' recommendations are not delivered from on high, but are rather the educated guesses of what decisions would be arrived at by a group of citizens engaged in proper *democratic deliberation*. One might alternatively claim that the expert's recommendations are based on evidence about what actually is in fact best (or at least better)

for human beings. Quite apart from any concerns about, for
example, one's (natural) right to decide a course of life for oneself, I do not believe these objections will ultimately overcome
the arguments that led Smith to adopt the political economy he
does. I will not burden the reader with my refutation of these
objections here, though I register the fact that Smith's position
puts him at odds with most of today's political theorists.[25]

I would, however, like to discuss briefly one objection to the
Smithian argument—namely that although experts might not
know the details of any given individual's values, opportunities,
resources, and so on, nevertheless what an intelligent third
party can know is not inconsiderable. It would include, for example, the general outlines of sound economic theory, the general
outlines of sound human biology, psychology, and nutrition, and
the general outlines of sound morality and thus politics. Even
Adam Smith evidently believes that general truths of morality,
economics, and jurisprudence can be known—why else would
he have written his two books, after all, if not to promulgate the
truths he believed he had uncovered? David Hume responded
to a similar claim in this way: "To balance a large state or society,
whether monarchical or republican, on general laws, is a work of
so great difficulty, that no human genius, however comprehensive, is able, by the mere dint of reason and reflection, to effect
it."[26] But that seems too flippant: surely economists, psycholo-
gists, philosophers, and political scientists have genuine expert
knowledge that can be exploited to guide sound policy.[27] Thus
perhaps we can reformulate the GMF in a way that might avoid
a fallacy. This new version would hold that experts have knowledge that enables them to make *more informed* decisions about
policy than people without expert knowledge can, and hence
letting experts make some decisions would lead to *better*, if not
perfect, outcomes than if we let individuals make decisions for
themselves. To deny even this claim risks implying, implausibly,
that these disciplines have no expert knowledge whatsoever.

The question of whether these disciplines count as proper
sciences is beyond our scope here,[28] but I believe we can marshal
a modest Smithian response to this claim. The Smithian argument allows for knowledge, or potential knowledge, of general
economic processes that can allow retrodiction but not precise
prediction. Evolutionary biology provides an analogy. Given
what biologists have been able to learn about the processes

involved in evolutionary descent, they can give plausible explanations for how any given species might have arrived, how it got to be where it is today, and why it succeeded where its competitors failed. They can also make general claims about what the future might be like, along the lines of: "any successful organism or species will need to have favorable biological, climatic, and ecological characteristics . . . ." What they cannot say, however, is exactly which species will survive in the future and which will not, what conditions will turn out to be favorable for any given species and what will not, or, with anything approaching certainty, what the effects will be of making even slight changes in ecosystems. The reason is that there is too much complexity and far too many variables involved.[29] Some, like naturalist E. O. Wilson, argue that one day even the social sciences will be brought into the proper science fold by basing their work on the advances in brain science and evolutionary biology and psychology, and ultimately on chemistry and physics. But even Wilson acknowledges that "The greatest challenge today, not just in cell biology and ecology but in all of science, is the accurate and complete description of complex systems" (Wilson 1999: 93). He continues: "At higher, more specific levels of organization, beyond the traditional realm of physics, the difficulties of synthesis are almost inconceivably more difficult. Entities such as organisms and species, unlike electrons and atoms, are indefinitely variable" (ibid., 94). A new discipline of economics attempting to bridge some of these gaps of complexity has arisen—"neuroeconomics"[30]—and it hopes to make economics a proper science by studying human brain activity, thereby enabling surer prediction of human behavior. Recent advances in brain science give this project some hope, but it must be acknowledged that it is a long way away from enabling predictions of any actual human beings in actual, real-world situations.

The Smithian would make an analogous claim about political economy: no legislator or philosopher can account for all, or even most, of the variables involved in designing an economy or a society. The variation in individual circumstances and the factors involved in human behavior exceed by orders of magnitude anyone's ability to manage or even know. Smith did not argue that markets solve all these problems, but his Economizer Argument and Local Knowledge Argument do entail that markets' decentralization, their dependence on uncoordinated individuals' decisions, and their sensitivity to changing local contexts allow the emergence of patterns of order whose conduciveness to people's general welfare will outstrip what any expert could have deliberately designed. The Economizer Argument and the Invisible Hand Argument even suggest a cautious optimism, as long as the "obvious and simple system of natural liberty" (WN IV.ix.51) is allowed to operate. By contrast, not even a group of "the best brains," as Schumpeter suggested (Schumpeter 1975 [1942]: 198), would be adequate to the task of deliberately directing this process: for they would neither be able to gather the appropriate information; nor able to effect real-time reckonings of whatever incomplete information they had, because constant changes in circumstances require constant reassessment; nor reliably manage human behavior because they do not yet have a competent understanding of the factors involved in human action. Despite the great advances in scientific knowledge, then—and the legitimate claims to expert knowledge—to believe these obstacles could be overcome would be, for Smith, still to commit the GMF.

The Seen and the Unseen

The nineteenth-century French economist Frédéric Bastiat (1801–50) argued that the difference between the good economist and the bad economist is that the latter pays attention only to the obvious and present results of policies and actions, whereas the former pays attention both to the obvious and present results *and* to the non-obvious and long-term results. In Bastiat's words, the bad economist pays attention only to what is "seen," while the good economist pays attention both to what is "seen" and to what is "unseen."[31] This surprisingly simple insight might strike one as indeed too simple: Who does not know, one might ask, that in weighing the costs and benefits, say, of a proposed economic policy, one must weigh *all* potential costs against the benefits, not only the initial and obvious costs? For otherwise the analysis is incomplete: weighing partial costs against full benefits stacks the deck. Perhaps almost everyone knows this in some sense, but few observe the maxim in practice: again and again economic policies are proposed that are justified only by what is "seen," without proper reckoning of the policy's "unseen" costs.

It turns out that Smith saw this danger, some three-quarters of a century before Bastiat. Smith expressed it in terms of what we might today call "opportunity cost," which can result from artificially directing capital flows into directions they would not "naturally" have followed.[32] Smith's assumptions are (1) resources are scarce, meaning that not all potential uses of resources can be pursued simultaneously; (2) choices must therefore be made that entail that resources are directed to some ends but not others; and (3) there is no third-party Great Mind that can know where all resources should be directed. The myriad directions in which capitals would flow if individuals are allowed the freedom to decide where to expend their own resources constitute, for Smith, the "natural flows" of capitals. By contrast, the artificial, or "unnatural," flows are those that are diverted from their natural directions by third-party interposition: trade barriers and tariffs, legally enforced monopolies, etc. Smith's argument in this passage in WN is thus that these unnatural flows may lead to present and obvious—"seen"—benefits, but what is not reckoned into the reasoning of the third-party interposers is what those resources might otherwise have done, if they had been allowed to follow their natural course. As Smith argues, without third-party interposition and redirection of capital flows,

> More houses would have been built, more lands would have been improved, and those which had been improved before would have been better cultivated, more manufactures would have been established, and those which had been established before would have been extended; and to what height the real wealth and revenue of the country might, by this time, have been raised, it is not perhaps very easy even to imagine. (WN II.iii.35)

These are all the "unseen" costs of intervention.

Hence quite apart from any consideration of whether the state should have the right to direct capital flows—that is, to tell individuals where they must or may not expend their limited resources—Smith's argument issues in two practical conclusions. First, policy-makers routinely bias their cost/benefit calculations in favor of their proposals by leaving out "unseen," but no less real, costs.[33] Second, because the proposed policies almost invariably involve the substitution of third-parties' judgment for the judgment of individuals with local knowledge, the policies stand little chance of having overall beneficial outcomes.

Instead, they will almost always benefit some small but "seen" group at the expense of a larger but "unseen" group. Smith's argument thus entails a strong presumption against third-party interposition in markets, and in favor of allowing them to ebb and flow freely.

The GMF and the Impartial Spectator

Smith's GMF also bears interestingly on his "impartial spectator" standard of morality. As we saw in Chapter 4, Smith presents in TMS the "impartial spectator" as a regulative ideal that not only captures how we actually pass moral judgments, but also provides a normative measuring stick by which to judge our own and others' actions. According to Smith, the assumption that people make moral judgments by consulting an imagined impartial spectator accounts for a large range of human moral behavior. In fact, Smith believes that the assumption that we consult, or believe we should consult, an impartial spectator explains far more than just "moral" behavior. Thus Smith offers in his *Lectures on Jurisprudence* an impartial spectator theory of property, and his "Considerations Concerning the First Formation of Languages" offers an explanation of language change and development that is consistent with, and even implies, the existence of an impartial spectator theory of language usage, although he does not explicitly mention it in the essay. Yet it might seem that Smith is committing his own version of the GMF: for who is this impartial spectator, and why are his determinations authoritative? Smith's use of the impartial spectator does not commit the GMF, however. Let me close this chapter by suggesting how what I call his "impartial spectator theory of property" in fact constitutes an instructive instance of his appreciation of the GMF.

In his lectures on jurisprudence, Smith begins his discussion of "private law" by listing five ways by which property is acquired—occupation, accession, prescription, succession, and voluntary transference.[34] Here is Smith on "occupation": "Occupation seems to be well founded when the *spectator* can go along with my possession of the object, and approve me when I defend my possession by force" (LJ, 459). Under "prescription," Smith says,

> There are four things requisite to form a right by prescription. 1st, bona fides, for if a person be sensible that his right to a

thing is bad it is no injury to deprive him of it, and the *indifferent spectator* can easily go along with the depriving him of the possession. (LJ, 461)

A few lines later, "If he claims a right [to property] without any such tittle no *impartial spectator* can enter into his sentiments" (LJ, 461). Later in the same report, where Smith is discussing the third kind of personal rights, namely "ex delicto," he says, "Injury naturaly excites the resentment of the *spectator*, and the punishment of the offender is reasonable as far as the *indifferent spectator* can go along with it. This is the natural measure of punishment" (LJ, 475). And when discussing the "right of accession," Smith says that it "is not so much founded in it's utility as in the *impropriety* of not joining to it that object on which it has a dependence" (LJ, 460)—a reference to the impartial spectator's role in determining propriety, as laid out in TMS.[35]

Thus what constitutes ownership, property, and proper punishment for transgression, according to Smith, is determined by what an "impartial" or "indifferent" spectator would adjudge. Crucially, however, Smith believes that there is no set of universal rules that uniquely and correctly determine these matters. Although we can articulate general principles, arrived at inductively on the basis of past experience, in any particular cases— especially to resolve disputes—we must instead consult an imagined impartial spectator, relying on his judgment to render decisions in concrete cases. According to Smith, the impartial spectator, or the judge imagining him, should, first, know the relevant details of the case, including the parties involved, their relevant history, the local customs or practices, and so on; and he should have no personal stake in the outcome of the case. Yet Smith believes that each of these issues requires interpretive judgment—to know which facts are relevant and which not, how the previous customs apply to this case, and so on. If interpretive judgment is always required, then the judge's routine judgments can best be explained as a (sometimes unconscious) consultation of the perspective of an impartial spectator. They can also be, and regularly are, criticized if they do not issue from or conform to such a perspective.

The application of any of the five ways by which Smith thinks one can get property will require interpretation and judgment. How long must one occupy land to become its rightful owner? Smith's answer: that length of time an impartial spectator would

judge necessary before approving of its occupant having title to
it. How long is that? Smith's answer: whatever a fully informed
but disinterested judge would approve. How in practice does
one determine what such a judge would approve? One must
approximate, in one's imagination, the perspective of a fully
informed but disinterested judge of the case at hand and ask
oneself what a person so situated would think. Smith's claim is
that there is no set of universal or *a priori* rules that will uniquely
determine the proper solution or settlement to every dispute.
What the judge has at his disposal is his knowledge of previous
case law, his knowledge of the particulars involved in the case
before him now, and, if he is a good judge, his sense of what, as
Smith says, is "reasonable" in such a situation.

Now "reasonableness" may seem to introduce something new
to the discussion, but in fact it is just Smith's adversion to the
impartial spectator. Smith relies on the notion of "reasonableness" time and again in LJ. For example:

> From the system I have already explain'd, you will remember
> that I told you we may conceive an injury was done when an
> *impartial spectator* would be of opinion he was injured, would
> join with him in his concern and go along with him when he
> defend<ed> the subject in his possession against any violent
> attack, or used force to recover what had been wrongfully
> wrested out of his hand. [. . .] The spectator would justify the
> first possessor in defending and even in avenging himself when
> injured, in the manner we mentioned. The cause of this sym-
> pathy or concurrence betwixt the spectator and the possessor
> is, that he enters into his thoughts and concurrs in his opinion
> that he may form a reasonable expectation of using the fruit
> or whatever it is in the manner he pleases. This expectation
> justifies in the mind of the spectator, the possessor both when
> he defends himself [. . .]. The *reasonable expectation* therefore
> which the first possessor furnishes is the ground on which the
> right of property is acquired by occupation. (LJ, 17)

When in LJ Smith recurs to the notion of "reasonableness" as a
criterion of adjudication, he typically puts it in terms of "reasonable expectations" on behalf of a property owner or a challenger,
the "reasonableness" being determined by the impartial spectator. For example: "That obligation to performance which arises

from contract is founded on the *reasonable expectation* produced by a promise, which considerably differs from a declaration of intention" (LJ, 472). What would make an expectation reasonable? Smith's answer is, again, that it is reasonable if an impartial spectator would approve of it. If the further question is asked where exactly the perspective of the impartial spectator comes from, his answer would be to look at parts I–III of TMS. There he lays out the "gradual" development of this perspective, beginning with the infant, who has no sense of propriety, proceeding to the "great school of self-command" (TMS III.3.22) that begins the child's process of development, then to the development of a generalized perspective, and finally to the creation of an imaginary and idealized impartial spectator that serves as one's conscience.[36] As we saw in Chapter 3, a given individual's imagined impartial spectator is based on generalizations that individual has drawn from his past experience of what other actual spectators (including himself) have approved or disapproved in various circumstances. We infer, inductively but often unconsciously, general habits and even principles of judging from the numerous particular instances of judgment we have experienced, correcting them according to their relative success at serving their purposes—usually to attain a "mutual sympathy of sentiments" (TMS I.1.2.1 and passim). We thus develop a generalized sense of what a fully informed but disinterested person would approve or disapprove in a case like the one before us, and this sense is what issues in the judgment of an impartial spectator.

Is the perspective of the impartial spectator infallible? No: it is based on the observations and generalizations of fallible human beings. Hence the Smithian impartial spectator is not the voice of God or any other Great Mind. It is instead the coalescence of fallible human judgments on the basis of limited human experience filtered through human biases and prejudices. The imagined impartial spectator's perspective is idealized, but it is an all-too-human construction whose worth is judged by its effectiveness, which itself is measured by human beings against human goals. It is thus more like Protagoras's "man is the measure of all things" than Plato's Forms, God's transcendent judgment, or the omniscience of a Great Mind. I suggest, then, that Smith's aversion to an impartial-spectator standard is not a commission of the GMF, but is instead consistent with the claim that the GMF is in fact a fallacy. According to the Smithian argument, what constitutes ownership, what constitutes property, and how disputes should be resolved are all matters for localized judgment. They can be aided by principles derived inductively on the basis of past experience, but in any particular case they will need supplementing by assessment of local facts performed by local judges. To believe, by contrast, that one can apprehend universal rules that establish the nature and scope of ownership and property and that will adjudicate all real-world disputes would, for Smith, be yet another instance of committing the GMF.

Notes

[1] Some, like Rashid (1998), are inclined to be rather harsher in their judgment of Smith's originality. Aspromourgos (2009) is a recent examination of Smith's sources and his relative originality.

[2] See Rousseau (1987 [1754]) and (2003 [1754]).

[3] For a penetrating critique of Rousseau's argument, see Hocutt (Fall 2003); for a recent discussion of the relation of Smith to Rousseau, see Rasmussen (2008).

[4] See, for example, WN Intro.4.

[5] See Peart and Levy (2005) and Sunstein (1997).

[6] The vagueness here is important. It would include, for example, the motivations of scientists who pursue their researches not for monetary gain but, as Smith argues in HA, for the love of truth. See Chapter 2.

[7] See Peart and Levy (2005).

[8] What follows is based on Otteson (2010a).

[9] See Nozick (1974), 160–4.

[10] Other statements of the Local Knowledge Argument can be found throughout WN. See, for example, WN I.i.8, IV.v.b.16, IV.v.b.25, and IV.ix.51.

[11] Smith also writes: "But though the profusion of government must, undoubtedly, have retarded the natural progress of England towards wealth and improvement, it has not been able to stop it. The annual produce of its land and labour is, undoubtedly, much greater at present than it was either at the restoration or at the revolution. The capital, therefore, annually employed in cultivating this land, and in maintaining this labor, must likewise be much greater. In the midst of all the exactions of government, this capital has been silently and gradually accumulated by *the private frugality and good conduct of individuals, by their universal, continual, and uninterrupted effort to better their own condition.* It is this effort, protected by law and allowed by liberty

to exert itself in the manner that is most advantageous, which has maintained the progress of England towards opulence and improvement in almost all former times, and which, it is to be hoped, will do so in all future times" (WN II.iii.36; my emphasis). This argument too can be found throughout WN. See, for example, WN I.viii.44, I.x.c.14, II.i.30, II.iii.28, II.iii.31, II.v.37, III.iii.12, IV.ii.4, IV.ii.8, IV.v.b.43, IV.ix.28, and V.i.b.18. See also LJ (A), vi.145.

[12] Many commentators get it wrong. Emma Rothschild, for example, describes the "invisible hand" passage in WN as an "ironic joke"; see Rothschild (2001), chapter 5. See also Kennedy (2008) and Craig Smith (2006).

[13] Smith continues: "Nor is it always the worse for the society that it was no part of it [that is, his intention]. By pursuing his own interest he frequently promotes that of the society much more effectually than when he really intends to promote it. I have never known much good done by those who affected to trade for the publick good" (WN IV.ii.9). Smith repeats variants of this argument throughout WN as well. See, for example, WN Introduction.8, II.Introduction.4, II. iii.39, IV.ii.4, IV.v.b.25, and IV.vii.c.88.

[14] In his 1793 *Account of the Life and Writings of Adam Smith, LL.D.*, Dugald Stewart speaks of a manuscript of Smith's, now unfortunately lost, that Stewart reports as stating, "Little else is requisite to carry a state to the highest degree of opulence from the lowest barbarism, but peace, easy taxes, and a tolerable administration of justice; all the rest being brought about by the natural course of things. All governments which thwart this natural course, which force things into another channel, or which endeavour to arrest the progress of society at a particular point, are unnatural, and to support themselves are obliged to be oppressive and tyrannical" (EPS IV.25).

[15] See Hayek (1980 [1945]), 77–91; and Hayek (1960), chapters 1 and 2.

[16] See TMS II.ii.1.9 and II.ii.2.2.

[17] Sunstein (1997), 26–9.

[18] Ibid., 30. Sunstein also asserts that "The American government should compile and distribute an annual 'quality of life' report, including, among other things, per capita income, poverty, housing, unemployment, average weekly earnings, inflation, child mortality, longevity, subjective to violent crime, literacy, and educational attainment. The report should also specify minimum standards for such things as income, education, health, and housing and allow for comparison across regions, between men and women, and among different racial and ethnic groups" (123). Knowing what should count as "minimum standards" for such matters is just the kind of thing that Smith would claim a legislator, however wise, cannot know.

[19] Thaler and Sunstein (2008).

[20] Ibid., 1–6, 103–31, and 67–8, respectively.

[21] For this and other examples, see Thaler and Sunstein (2008), 68, 72, 80, 127, 155, and 192.

[22] See ibid., chapter 18 and passim.

[23] This claim is illustrated by the broad scope of other topics Thaler and Sunstein discuss, including prescription drugs, environmental and energy issues, organ donation, schooling and education, health care and medical lotteries, and marriage unions and partnerships. See Thaler and Sunstein (2008), chapters 10–15.

[24] Ubel (2009), for example, extends Thaler and Sunstein's argument to press for more extensive "expert" guidance and curtailment of individual choices.

[25] For an extended discussion, see Otteson (2010a).

[26] Hume (1987 [1741]), 124.

[27] I note that Sunstein has been named by President Obama the "Administrator of the White House Office of Information and Regulatory Affairs"—or, as it is more popularly known, the "Regulation Czar."

[28] See, for example, Veblen (2008 [1899]) and Kahneman and Tversky (2000). Ubel makes use of Kahneman and Tversky's work to criticize supporters of free markets; see Ubel (2009), chapters 1 and 3.

[29] The failed Biosphere experiments are cases in point. See *New York Times* (November 19, 1996 and September 9, 2003).

[30] For an overview, see Camerer (March 2007).

[31] See Bastiat (1995 [1850]).

[32] For Smith on opportunity cost, see, for example, WN II.ii.35–6. On "natural" versus "artificial" capital flows, see, for example, WN III.i.8–9, IV.ii.3, and IV.ix.50–1.

[33] See also WN V.iii., in which Smith discusses the dangers of public debt, another species of "unseen" cost.

[34] LJ, 459. All emphases in the quotations from LJ are mine. Note that the LJ students' notes of Smith's lectures, not Smith's own notes.

[35] There are additional references to impartial or indifferent spectators in LJ. See, for example, LJ, 17, 19, 32, 87, and 104.

[36] See Campbell (1971), chapter 6; Otteson (2002), chapters 1–3; and Craig Smith (2006), chapters 3 and 7.

Chapter 7

Resolving the "Adam Smith Problem"

By the time August Oncken published his seminal article in 1897,[1] the scholarly tide was already turning regarding the so-called Adam Smith Problem. During the previous half-century or so, several commentators had pressed what German scholars called the *Umschwungstheorie*, which held that Adam Smith the moral philosopher, who in *The Theory of Moral Sentiments* (TMS) thought that human relations were based on a "sympathy" people felt for one another, at some point became Adam Smith the economist, who in *The Wealth of Nations* (WN) thought that "self-love" was what motivated people. A series of nineteenth-century scholars had argued that there were, after all, two Adam Smiths, not one, and they duly conferred on this alleged inconsistency the honorific "Das Adam Smith Problem." Smith had produced several editions of TMS during his lifetime, including a final, substantially revised edition only months before he died (and thus some 15 years after the first publication of WN): How could one take Smith seriously if he failed to realize his own fundamental conversion in philosophical outlook, even while revising the books side by side? Perhaps Smith was a great economist, some nineteenth-century scholars sniffed, but he was no philosopher.

By the close of the nineteenth century, however, several works had appeared that argued for Smith's consistency after all. Principal among these were John Rae's *Life of Adam Smith* and Edwin Cannan's publication of a student's notes from Smith's lectures on jurisprudence.[2] On the basis of these works, August Oncken argued that the Adam Smith Problem should be put to rest. The earlier scholars thought that Smith had undergone a radical change of mind while in France in the mid-1760s, specifically when he visited Helvetius and other Physiocrats[3] in

Paris in 1766. TMS had first come out in 1759, and we know that
Smith had begun work on WN almost immediately after returning from Paris.[4] The nineteenth-century scholars argued that
TMS was written by a bright though naïve young man who, still
under the influence of his teacher, Francis Hutcheson, believed
in human benevolence and sympathy. After living with the Physiocrats for a year, however, Smith's worldview hardened as he
came to believe that it was "self-love," not benevolence, that
drove human beings. WN, then, is the result of this change in
perspective, and man's self-love accordingly founds the argument in WN.

This story was in an important respect factually incorrect, as
Oncken pointed out. Smith had been lecturing on jurisprudence for several years prior to his trip to Paris, and the content
of these lectures, as Cannan and Rae had discovered, revealed
that the core of WN already occupied a significant place in
Smith's thought concerning jurisprudence. Whatever else hap-
pened in Paris in 1766, Smith's visit did not cause him to change
his mind. He seemed to have developed the ideas for WN on his
own, and he was doing so about the same time he was preparing
the second edition of TMS.[5]

Over the course of the twentieth, and now into the twenty-
first, century, the issue of whether there is a real "Adam Smith
Problem," and if so what its true nature is, has enjoyed a great
deal of spilt scholarly ink.[6] Surveying all the versions of the Adam
Smith Problem that scholars have pressed, along with their various solutions and objections to one another's solutions, is
beyond the scope of this book. Instead I propose to sketch one
way that TMS and WN are deeply connected. As I have suggested
earlier, I believe that early in his career Smith conceived of a
model for explaining large-scale human social institutions, and
that much of his extant work—including in particular TMS and
WN—evinces his methodical attempts to explore the application of this model to successive areas of human social life.

In this chapter, then, I begin with a brief reminder of this
model's presence in Smith's early essay on the origins of languages. I then show how the model appears and is articulated in
TMS and then in WN. If I am right that this model persists
throughout Smith's major works, then this fact would, I submit,
constitute a step toward resolving the so-called Adam Smith
Problem.

The Model in Smith's Essay on Language

Smith's "Languages" appeared in 1761 in the journal *The Philological Miscellany*. Although the date of this essay's publication is 2 years after the first publication of TMS in 1759, it was apparently in the works before Smith began preparations of what was to become TMS. The chronology is important because the model revealed by Smith's analysis in "Languages" is also to be found in TMS, and, by the time Smith writes TMS, it has become for him the key to understanding the nature of moral judgment and moral standards, as well as the nature of human association generally. "Languages" reveals only the rudiments of this model, but as Smith matured he increasingly drew on these rudiments to explain more and more human behavior.

As we saw in Chapter 2, Smith begins "Languages" with a "conjectural history" of the formation of languages that asserts that two savages "who had never been taught to speak, but had been bred up remote from the societies of men, would naturally begin to form that language by which they would endeavour to make their mutual wants intelligible to each other" (LRBL, 203).[7] Smith's savages begin by giving names to particular things they find in their immediate surroundings—that is, things with which they become familiar. As they discover, however, that the particular things they have denominated "cave," "tree," and "fountain" resemble other objects as well, they "naturally bestow, upon each of these new objects, the same name by which they had been accustomed to express the similar object they were first acquainted with" (ibid.).[8]

Smith's analysis entails a lack of conscious direction for overall linguistic development. Proper nouns get transformed into common nouns by an unconscious process of mental association triggered by the expanding range of experience people had as they evolved from savages to cosmopolitan eighteenth-century Scots. Enlarged experience brings with it an increasing number of things that require names. Their desires naturally expand with their expanded experience, gradually leading the savages to expand the usage of their proper nouns and create those terms we call general names. Thus the development of language presupposes no conscious direction. The savages did not decide in advance how to make their language more sophisticated; instead, its sophistication arose as their needs required.

The fact that this natural formation of language happens without conscious deliberation does not mean it happens lawlessly or haphazardly. Rules for the use of words are formed even as the words themselves are formed: this word, pronounced precisely in this way, means this; that word, pronounced in that way, means that. The rules initially constitute informally agreed-upon protocols; in time they become formal rules that get taught to children and sometimes written down as the rules of grammar. The notes from Lecture 3 in LRBL report Smith as having said that the rules form by "mutual consent" (9, §18), but that should not be construed to mean that the savages worked out a plan or strategy for the development of language in advance and then all agreed to follow it. This would be a circular explanation: assuming a linguistic and conceptual sophistication in order to explain the creation of this same sophistication. The "mutual consent" would instead be on-the-spot and spontaneous; the newly agreed-to usage would then gain a wider currency only if it proved to be an efficient way to satisfy the savages' wants. The "consent" would come about de facto on the actual employment of the new usage:

> When there was occasion, therefore, to mention any particular object, it often became necessary to distinguish it from the other objects comprehended under the same general name, either, first, by its peculiar qualities; or, secondly, by the peculiar relation which it stood in to some other things. (LRBL, 205)

A desire to communicate some specific new need pressured the savages into creating a peculiarly apt expression. As needs changed, so did language; but changing language as an ordered system was not part of anyone's intention.

As we discussed in Chapter 2, Smith thinks that no person or group of persons devised the rules of grammar *ex nihilo* and handed them down like ukases to the masses; on the contrary, the rules of particular languages are devised and revised on the basis of induction on current and long-standing usage. The usage comes first, the rules only later. New usages and variations continually change and develop language, "without," as Smith puts it, "any intention or foresight in those who first set the example, and who never meant to establish any general rule"

(LRBL, 211). "The general rule would establish itself insensibly, and by slow degrees, in consequence of that love of analogy and similarity of sound, which is the foundation of by far the greater part of the rules of grammar" (ibid.). This description is thus reminiscent of the passage in WN in which Smith speaks of the "invisible hand" that ensures that people's self-interested economic pursuits also conduce to the overall welfare of society.[9] There is, of course, no real hand, which is why Smith calls it "invisible." It is instead a metaphor standing for no conscious or intentional thing at all: it is a consequence unintended by individuals that their self-interested actions raise the overall standard of living.[10] Although the chains of events that link individual actions to general welfare can be traced after the fact, general welfare was not part of the individuals' intention or design; as far as the individuals are concerned, the two are connected by sheer coincidence. Smith makes a similar point when he writes that general rules of grammar establish themselves "insensibly." It may be difficult to accept the possibility that an elaborate, sophisticated institution—like a language—could have developed with no overall rational design, but Smith, prefiguring Darwin, thinks that natural human languages are precisely such unplanned systems, and this is his point in saying that the rules of grammar arise "insensibly."

Thus for Smith language is created, changed, and revised by individuals who have no grand scheme in mind. They use it as a means to achieve other ends, and they change it as their ends change, without a thought as to what their changes mean for the "system" of language. As their range of experiences outgrows their limited capacity to know all objects as particulars, the complexity and sophistication of their language grows accordingly.[11] The changes that occur in language take place insensibly, and people's needs change slowly enough to allow general rules of the language to unfold, be formalized, and perhaps get written down. Moreover, the sustaining and changing of the language depends on a continuous, free exchange of words and usage. The history of languages shows that as peoples and nations come into contact with one another and associate in various ways, languages change accordingly to accommodate the new people, ideas, and ways—but not as a result of central, authoritative commands. People using the languages change them as the need to do so arises. And all this is brought about by individuals' various desires and their quest to find means to satisfy those desires. The result is a system of "spontaneous order": a self-enforcing, orderly institution created unintentionally by the free exchanges of individuals who desire only to satisfy their own individual wants.

The Model in TMS

As we saw in Chapter 3, Smith offers a market-model for the development of human morality. According to his explanation, babies begin with nothing but wants, with no tincture of remorse, shame, or guilt at wanting something improper. As babies grow into children, they have the first experience of discipline, which teaches them that others judge them and expect them to behave in particular ways; their desire for mutual sympathy of sentiments (MSS) encourages them to learn what others expect of them and to strive to achieve it. The more experience they have, the better they become at anticipating others' expectations and hence of behaving in ways that lead to MSS. The children then develop habits of behavior that reflect what they have learned. In time the habits can become internalized principles by which the children routinely order their lives. As adults, larger experience has led to more, and more complicated, principles, covering a large range of actions and motivations, and they have been revised, corrected, and fine-tuned as necessary. These principles come to inform the perspective of an impartial spectator, which provides the standard against which people judge themselves and others.

As in "Languages," in TMS Smith argues that moral judgments, along with the rules by which we render them, also develop without an overall plan. They arise and grow into a public system of morality—meaning a general consensus regarding the nature of propriety and merit—on the basis of countless individual judgments made in countless particular situations. As Smith had argued that the complexity of language increases as our experience grows, in TMS Smith argues that enlarged experience as we grow from infants to children to adults leads to the development of increasingly sophisticated principles of judgment enabling us to assess and evaluate an increasingly diverse range of actions and motivations. Smith had argued that the changes in language that lead to its formalization came about "insensibly" and "by slow degrees"; precisely the same, he argues in TMS, is the case with the development of the general rules of morality and judgment that we form. What seem when we are children to be haphazard interactions with others lead, as we grow older, to habits of behavior; as adults the habits solidify into principles that guide our conscience. Smith had argued that the similarities in our experiences was enough to allow for rules of language to be formalized, recorded, and taught; yet over long periods of time languages change significantly, as individuals' experiences change. The development of moral standards is the same. People's interests, experiences, and environments change slowly enough to allow long-standing associations and institutions to arise, giving a firm foundation to the rules, standards, and protocols that support these associations and in turn are supported by them. Religious orders, legal codes, and numerous cultural practices manifest and propound a community's moral standards, and these standards will last as long as those institutions and practices enjoy the reverence of the community's members—which, of course, is not forever, just as no language remains in use forever.

Smith had suggested in "Languages" that the progress and development of language depended on a continuous, open exchange of words. In TMS, Smith argues that the development of personal moral standards, of a conscience and perspective of the impartial spectator, and of the accepted moral standards of a community all depend on the regular associations people make with one another. In the daily intercourse people have with one another they encourage each other to discover and adopt rules of behavior and judgment that will lead to mutual sympathy. Without such interactions with others—recall the case of the solitary islander—people would have no occasion to pursue such rules, and hence they would not. In that case moral judgments would not be made at all, and people would not, as the solitary man does not, have thoughts about virtue or vice, propriety or impropriety. Finally, Smith had argued that the development of language ultimately came about as result of desires people have, desires that language, as a tool by which people could organize and cooperate, better enabled them to satisfy. Again the same holds true for the system of moral judgments. Rather than the desire for food, shelter, or clothing, the desire that motivates a person's (largely unconscious) adoption of general rules is the desire for mutual sympathy. I have called this desire the *sine qua non* for Smith's theory of moral sentiments, and here we can see why: without it, there would have been no reason to devise rules that enable people to achieve it, and, on Smith's account, there would therefore have been no moral standards at all—in the same way that if each person could completely supply all his own wants and needs there would quite likely have been no language, either.

The Model in WN

The model Smith articulates in "Languages," then, is used and elaborated in TMS. Yet Smith's writings on the development of economic markets in WN reveal that he found this realm of human experience also to adhere to the model he had found in the realm of human language. All three—language, morality, and economics—are systems of unintended order: they all develop according to and conform to the model of a *market*.

The notion that in WN Smith thought that the relatively unimpeded operation of markets leads to systems of unintended order is perhaps more obvious and less controversial than that he thought something similar in TMS or in "Languages." Let me, then, mention only a few elements of Smith's analysis in WN that indicate its adherence to the same model.

People find, make, and acquire various things, and if left to their own devices they will trade some of them with other people for other things. These exchanges are generally mutually advantageous: each party to the transaction trades a possession of his for the possession of someone else, which each person values more than he values what he already has.[12]

> But man has almost constant occasion for the help of his brethren, and it is in vain for him to expect it from their benevolence only. He will be more likely to prevail if he can interest their self-love in his favour, and shew them that it is for their own advantage to do for him what he requires of them. Give me that which I want, and you shall have this which you want, is the meaning of every such offer; and it is in this manner that we obtain from one another the far greater part of those good offices which we stand in need of. (WN I.ii.2)

Since we all have interests, desires, and needs, we seek ways to satisfy them through either production or barter. And since most of us cannot satisfy all our own needs, desires, and interests alone, each of us must barter to satisfy at least some of them. As it turns out that we all have peculiar talents, we tend to seek out our talents and to capitalize on them to maximize our advantage in exchanges of goods.

> And thus the certainty of being able to exchange all that surplus part of the produce of his own labour, which is over and above his own consumption, for such parts of the produce of other men's labour as he may have occasion for, encourages every man to apply himself to a particular occupation, and to cultivate and bring to perfection whatever talent or genius he may possess for that particular species of business. (WN I.ii.3)

With freedom to exchange and security in our possessions we will tend to focus our energies on tasks that we are good at, in the hopes of creating more of it than we ourselves need. This surplus we barter with others for other things that we want or need. Because everyone focuses himself in the same way and for the same reason, the supply of various goods in society gradually rises, accompanied by a gradual lowering of prices. The result is that more and more people can afford more and more things. Thus Smith writes:

> It is the great multiplication of the productions of all the different arts, in consequence of the division of labour, which occasions, in a well-governed society, that universal opulence which extends itself to the lowest ranks of people. Every workman has a great quantity of his own work to dispose of beyond what he himself has occasion for; and every other workman being exactly in the same situation, he is enabled to exchange a great quantity of his own goods for a great quantity, or, what comes to the same thing, for the price of a great quantity of theirs. He supplies them abundantly with what they have occasion for, and a general plenty diffuses itself through all of the different ranks of society. (WN I.i.10)

As we saw in Chapter 6, the qualification "in a well-governed society" is important. Smith shows that under the right conditions human economic systems tend over time to result in marketplaces of ever-widening scope. And he argues that as markets expand, productivity and supply of goods goes up, and hence prices go down. But what are the right conditions that allow the expansion of markets and resulting increase in material prosperity? Smith gives what one might call a natural history of human society, indicating that its four natural stages—hunting, shepherding, agriculture, and commerce[13]—are coincident with, and perhaps dependent upon, the gradual development of certain principles of exchange that tend to conduce to greater productivity. These principles generally tend to center around three things: individual liberty to dispose of oneself and one's belongs as one sees fit, protection of one's private property, and the sanctity of voluntary contractual agreements.[14] The principles begin informally, but in time they develop into full-fledged codes of behavior that can get written into law, adopted into "common law" judicial codes, or both. In LJ, Smith writes that government "arose, not as some writers imagine from any consent or agreement of a number of persons to submit themselves to such or such regulations, but from the natural progress which men make in society" (LJ, 207).

Smith's societal history shows that the absence of a controlling authority over people's economic lives does not result in anarchy, but rather in the development of relatively orderly systems of exchange—that is, in markets. What drives markets and determines what gets produced, at what cost and quantity, etc., is people's private wants and their spontaneous attempts to satisfy those wants by coordinating their efforts with others. The freedom to find ways to satisfy our wants does not produce anarchy, Smith believes, because even in the absence of externally enforced restrictions there arise practices, customs, and protocols as results of the ways individual people come to behave in their individual associations with one another.[15] Like the general rules of morality, the laws that get passed to regulate markets, including those defining and restricting private property and contracts, come on the heels of practices already established. We do not *a priori* define private property and then apply it to our community in the form of laws. Rather, the laws reflect what has already become the commonly accepted understanding, the prepollent (although not, of course, unanimous) consensus. This is the genesis of the unintended order of human society, and the historical explanation of those rules and laws that have developed in communities over the centuries.[16]

Smith did not believe that this slow development over time is uniformly good development. As we saw in Chapter 6, according to Smith the beneficial progress is often slowed and even reversed by vested interests, entrenched bureaucracies, or government-business partnerships to plunder some for the sake of others. In TMS, WN, and LJ Smith recounts several instances in which these problems and others impede society's progress toward greater material prosperity and beneficial laws.[17] Hence Donald Winch is correct that we should not ascribe to Smith a blind "sunny optimism" that markets will always and everywhere produce a beneficial "spontaneous harmony."[18] Moreover, it is of course true that, as commentators like Lionel Robbins, Jacob Viner, and Joseph Cropsey have maintained, Smithian markets require quite a bit of artificial regulative assistance to operate smoothly.[19] Thus Smith was not so naïve that he thought that markets would be perfect, or could be everything to everyone. His view was, as these commentators remind us, far more skeptical and realistic than that.

But a few things must be said. First, Smith's general skepticism about politics, which Winch rehearses with great care, is in fact a product of his belief that unplanned market-style institutions do a better job of eliciting practices and protocols that conduce to human benefit than could centrally planned political programs. Hence, contrary to the implication Winch draws, I think the two are quite consistent.[20] Moreover, although the rules defining marketplaces are artificial, that does not mean that they are not still explained by Smith's market model: like language, they still arose on the basis of on-the-spot trial-and-error, without any antecedent, overall plan. To repeat a passage cited a moment ago, Smith claims that government "arose, not as some writers imagine from any consent or agreement of a number of persons who submit themselves to such and such regulations, but from the natural progress which men make in society" (LJ, 207). He continues:

I showed how at first there was properly no government at all, that this arose first amongst a nation of shepherds, and that these in certain circumstances would naturally unite themselves and form a city, which at first was under the government of a chief, but afterwards became in the ordinary and naturall progress of things an aristocracy and afterwards a democracy. (LJ, 228)

Finally, despite his keen awareness of the glitches, backslidings, and disruptions to which the commentators point, Smith nevertheless saw the overall market-style development of human social institutions as beneficial, and thus the overall momentum of mankind's progress as being toward good—as shown in particular by his ultimate preference for the "obvious and simple system of natural liberty" (WN IV.ix.51). Smith's belief is that these institutions developing according to the market model do in the end progress beneficially, despite the inevitable problems that periodically arise.[21]

As I have said, Smith thinks that human beings have developed through four stages of society, each marked by increasing formalization of rules protecting "the laws of justice" and, to the extent that they allowed "the obvious and simple system of natural liberty" (WN IV.ix.51),[22] by increasing material prosperity as well. Smith's description of the progress of human society through these four stages contains several important features. First, the development was effected by individual people acting in conjunction with one another but without their intending to effect any overall development. Here Smith's notion of the "invisible hand" again plays an important role: people enter into various relationships with others in the market, and these relationships taken together constitute a larger system of a generally beneficial marketplace; but they did not intend to constitute the larger system.[23] Second, the development came about gradually and proceeded from informal to formal as people's needs and interests dictated. This feature is evident in Smith's description of the passage of various communities through the four stages, each of which is marked by increasingly complicated and formal rules regulating their conduct. Third, the development depends on regular associations and exchanges among individuals. This indeed is the immediate constituent of markets, the trucking, bartering, and exchanging of one thing for another that Smith thinks inevitably happens when people are left to their own devices. Finally, the development was initially and has continued to be motivated by the desires of the people within those societies. Put generally, this is the ever-present desire each of us has, as Smith puts it in WN, to better his own condition.[24] This single passage from near the beginning of WN contains early hints of all of these features:

This division of labour, from which so many advantages are derived, is not originally the effect of any human wisdom, which foresees and intends that general opulence to which it gives occasion. It is the necessary, though very slow and gradual consequence of a certain propensity in human nature which has in view no such extensive utility; the propensity to truck, barter, and exchange one thing for another. (WN I.ii.1)[25]

One final point about Smithian economic markets. A distinction should be drawn between the concept of a market on the one hand and actual marketplaces on the other. The concept of a market with which I argue Smith works is the theoretical model of a system of free exchange in which rules of exchange spontaneously develop. Marketplaces are the particular instantiations of this model that one finds virtually everywhere. The core features of Smithian marketplaces for the exchange of goods are protections of individual liberty, of private property, and of voluntary contracts, but all the other features one finds in any particular marketplace—which may include forms of address, codes of behavior, protocols of attire, even customs about precisely what counts as property and what counts as a contract[26]—will be heavily influenced by the traditions and practices of the particular peoples who are parties to the exchange. Even within a single community, there will be various orders or suborders of protocols that will display variations on the basic theme of a market. For example, the protocols of exchange at a contemporary suburban shopping mall are not the same as those in an auction at Sotheby's in New York, are not the same as those at a baseball card show, and are not the same as those at a farmer's market in any of a number of American cities. These are all marketplaces that to varying extents fit the general model of a market, but each displays its own concrete accidental features that reflect its place, time, and members. This feature of economic marketplaces parallels Smith's analysis of morality in TMS when he claims there that the "custom and fashion" of a particular place and time affect only the less important matters of, for example, manners, but not the substance of the central moral notions of propriety and merit (TMS V.2).

Smith's Market Model in Language, Economics, and Morals

The central structural elements of this "market model" can be mapped onto all three of Smith's works in this way:

1. Motivating Desire:

   (i) "Languages": the desire to make "mutual wants intelligible to each other" (LRBL, 203).

   (ii) TMS: the "pleasure of mutual sympathy" of sentiments (TMS I.i.2.1 and passim).

   (iii) WN: the "natural effort of every individual to better his own condition" (WN IV.v.b.43; cp. I.ii.2, II.iii.28, and II. iii.31).

2. Rules Developed:

   (i) "Languages": rules of grammar, pronunciation, usage, etc.

   (ii) TMS: standards of moral judgment and rules determining propriety and merit.

   (iii) WN: the "laws of justice" (WN IV.v.b.43; cp. LJ, 228 and 404–41), including protocols protecting private property, contractual agreements, and voluntary exchanges.

3. Currency (that is, what gets exchanged):

   (i) "Languages": words, ideas, and wants.

   (ii) TMS: personal sentiments and moral judgments.

   (iii) WN: goods and services.

4. Resulting "Unintended System of Order":

   (i) "Languages": language.

   (ii) TMS: commonly shared standards of morality and moral judgment.

   (iii) WN: economy (that is, large-scale network of exchanges of goods and services).

   I believe that an examination of Smith's works—not only TMS and WN, but also LJ and HA—reveals that the market model informed Smith's understanding of many other aspects of human life as well, including the development of governmental bodies, the development of notions of crime and proper punishment, the development of the institution of marriage, the development of science and scientific method, even the development of religious and educational institutions.[27] On this basis I therefore propose the larger claim that Smith saw his market model as the key to understanding the creation, development, and maintenance of human social life generally.

The market model would also seem to resolve the "Adam Smith Problem": If the same market-model that was present in Smith's early essay on languages also informed the analyses in both TMS and WN, then the central parts of Smith's corpus are, on a deep level, united.

Notes

[1] Oncken (1897).

[2] Rae (1895); Cannan (1896).

[3] For a discussion of the Physiocrats and their relation to Smith, see Muller (1993), 77–83.

[4] See Ross (1995), 220–47, and Rae (1895), 194–260.

[5] The second edition of TMS was published in 1761. Some manuscript fragments from what was to become WN exist and are thought to date from the early 1760s; these fragments are reprinted in LJ, 562–86.

[6] I too have contributed to the deluge: see Otteson (2000) and Otteson (2002), chapters 4 and 5. For a sampling, see Göçmen (2007), Montes (2004), Nieli (1986), Paganelli (2008), Viner (1928), and Young (1997).

[7] The story is repeated in the notes from Smith's third lecture on rhetoric, dated "Monday Nov. 22" of 1762, LRBL, 9–13.

[8] See Berry (1974).

[9] WN IV.ii.9.

[10] Thus Smith's invisible hand is not the same as the "hidden hand" some have argued explains, for example, the progress of science. See Hull (1988) and Way (March 2000).

[11] See LRBL, 217.

[12] See WN III.i.1; see also LJ, 511.

[13] Smith's notion of the four stages of human social evolution is a leitmotiv throughout WN. It is first broached in Smith's "Introduction and Plan of the Work," and it is especially apparent in bk. v, chapter 1.

[14] See WN II.i.30, II.iii.36, III.iii.12, III.iv.4, IV.v.b.43.

[15] See LJ, 18–37 and 207–15.

[16] See LJ, 404–41 and 460.

[17] See, for example, TMS II.iii.3.3–9, V.2.12–16, VI.ii.2.13–18, and VII. iv.34–7; see WNI.vii.26–8, I.viii.13, I.x.c.27, I.x.c.61, II.iii.28–31, II. iii.36–42, and II.v.7; and see LJ, 228–40, 521–41, and passim.

[18] Winch (1978), 176.

[19] Viner (1928), Robbins (1952), and Cropsey (1957).

[20] See Winch (1978), chapters 7 and 8.

[21] For passages that express Smith's optimism about the course of human progress, despite his general skepticism about politics, see WN I.xi.g–h, II.iii.33–6, IV.ix.50–1, V.i.f.25, and V.i.g.38; and LJ, 207–34, 486–7, and 539. For a view of Smith sympathetic to my own, see Macfarlane (2000), esp. chapter 6; for one that differs, see Rothschild (2001), esp. chapters 3, 5, and 8.

[22] For a discussion of the connection Smith sees between liberty and the rules of justice, see LJ, 275–82.

[23] See WN IV.ii.4–11.

[24] See WN II.iii.28, II.iii.31, II.iii.36, II.v.37, III.iii.12, IV.ii.4, and IV.ix.28.

[25] See also WN II.iii.36–9 and LJ, 351.

[26] See LJ, 71–6.

[27] Kennedy (2008: 37–48) offers a reconstruction and extension of my argument for a unity of the Smithian project. See esp. his chart on 42–3.

Part III

Enduring Significance

Chapter 8

What Smith Got Wrong

In this chapter and the next, we turn to assessing the contemporary significance of Adam Smith's work. In my judgment, Smith is one of the great philosophical figures of the Western tradition. Note that I said *philosophical* figures: His significance goes well beyond what falls within the purview of "economics" today, as I hope the previous chapters have attested. Yet no thinker, however great, got everything right. So what did Smith get right? What did he get wrong? In this chapter we take up the latter, in the next the former.

The two major things Smith seemed to have gotten wrong that we will discuss here are: (1) his labor theory of value and (2) his claim, at least in *The Theory of Moral Sentiments* (TMS), that happiness is connected to or perhaps consists in tranquility. At the end of the chapter we will take up an objection to Smith that I will argue does not ultimately hold up.

Labor Theory of Value

In chapters 4 and 5 of book 1 of *The Wealth of Nations* (WN), Smith outlines a theory of value that famously ties it to human labor. Smith identifies something he calls a "real price," which is determined by or reflects the amount of *labor* that is required to make something:

> The real price of everything, what every thing really costs to the man who wants to acquire it, is the toil and trouble of acquiring it. What every thing is really worth to the man who has acquired it, and who wants to dispose of it or exchange it for something else, is the toil and trouble which it can save to himself, and which it can impose upon other people. What is

bought with money or with goods is purchased by labour as much as what we acquire by the toil of our own body. That money or those goods indeed save this toil. (WN I.v.2)

Smith wishes to measure a thing's value by an objective standard, but the criterion he chooses, "labour," unfortunately fails to do the job—and many commentators have taken him to task for it.[1]

The consensus among economists today is that an attempt to understand value in terms of labor is confused. One of the central discoveries that led to modern economics was what is called the *subjective theory of value*—the notion that a thing's value cannot be sought in the thing itself or in any objective criterion or standard, but, rather, in what an individual is willing to sacrifice in order to get it. This notion of value allows us to understand otherwise paradoxical phenomena. For example, two people with the same amount of money may make different judgments about whether a product they are contemplating is worth the price. I may be willing to spend $5,000 for an autographed Babe Ruth baseball, but you would not; one employer might be willing to pay a worker only $10 per hour while another employer is willing to pay the same worker $15 per hour. What accounts for the differences? The mistake is to think that there is some objective value in the baseball or work that the prices are trying to approximate. On the contrary, discrepancies in judgments about what things are worth reflect the fact that a thing's value is determined by whatever a person is willing to give up for it. The Babe Ruth baseball is worth at least than $5,000 to me, for example, but less than that to you; the worker's time is worth only $10 per hour to one employer, but $15 to another. The values in each case are determined by the valuing agent, not the valued object. Hence the name "subjective value."

Although labor had seemed to Smith—and, later, to Marx—promising as an objective criterion of value, examination has revealed that it contains a host of problems. Labor is difficult to measure, and it varies from person to person: two people who worked for the same amount of time on something might not have expended the same amount of "labor," and it might take different people different amounts of "labor" to create precisely the same thing. Moreover, a labor theory of value has some recalcitrantly odd results: in easily imaginable cases it can turn out that a person expended a great deal of labor on something most people would agree is worthless. And what do we do about the location of a thing's value? Do we say that the labor creates value *in* a thing, meaning that the thing is what is now valuable, not the labor? Would this mean that an idle person is without value? Or do we say that labor itself is what is valuable? Then what is the metaphysical operation by which the labor infuses itself into an object?[2] When I buy a painting from Jones, am I not buying a painting, not Jones's "labor"? If it was Jones's labor that had value, however, then his labor must somehow be *in* the painting. But how, and what is the metaphysical entity that is or contains the value as it is being transferred?

In the latter part of the nineteenth century, thinkers who came to form the "Austrian School" of economics argued that the notion of inherent value imbued in an object by labor was incoherent.[3] In its stead, they set out the detailed and systematic case of their new discovery, the principle of diminishing marginal utility (PDMU), and the subjective theory of value it entailed. The PDMU holds that for any good or service a person wants, the $n + 1$st unit he receives is *ceteris paribus* less valuable to him than the nth unit.[4] This principle is based on the observation that people tend to put the first unit of any good or service to what they judge to be its most important use, the second unit to its second most important use, and so on, until eventually another unit is worth practically or actually nothing to them. Think of glasses of water for a thirsty person: the first is worth a great deal to him, the second is worth less, and so on, until, say, the fifth glass is worth nothing to him; perhaps the first two glasses he himself drinks, the third he gives to you, the fourth he uses to water his plant, and the fifth he dumps out.

What is important about the PDMU for our purposes is that it posits individual valuation. It shows that human beings value things based on personal preferences, and this valuation is what creates and fixes a thing's value. As Christian von Ehrenfels (1859–1932) argued, "we do not desire things because we grasp in them some mystical, incomprehensible essence 'value'; rather, we ascribe 'value' to things because we desire them."[5] Thus there is no "just" price, as for example St. Thomas Aquinas argued in the thirteenth century, and no "intrinsic" price, as for example Richard Cantillon argued in the eighteenth.[6] In fact a single thing can have indefinitely many values at the same time, each indexed to a particular valuing agent. Because the use to which a thing will be put is determined by an individual's unique circumstances and his unique schedule of preferences, it makes no sense to speak of one person's valuation of the thing applying to another person: even if two people in a particular case are willing to sacrifice the same amount for something, their respective valuations result from calculations based on different variables; hence one's valuation cannot substitute for the other's (and no third party's valuation can substitute for either of the other's). It follows that the value of the thing to one person cannot be compared to its value to the other.

Each act of valuation is relative, then, to a particular agent. That means that not only might two agents value a given thing at different rates, but they might value it relative to other things differently. So I value the Babe Ruth baseball more than you do, but we both value it more than, say, a mincemeat pie (which neither of us likes); that means we would both trade a mincemeat pie for the baseball. But how many mincemeat pies would we be willing to give up for a Babe Ruth baseball? I would presumably give up more than you, but how many more? The subjective theory of value says that there is no single "objectively correct" answer to how many should be traded, and that there is no way to calculate an exact value of a Babe Ruth baseball based on the number of mincemeat pies, because people do not judge value in terms of an objectively quantifiable criterion. They judge, rather, on the basis of their unique set of preferences, as driven by their present desires. Thus the actual value of the baseball to me may not only differ from the value of the baseball to you, but because our respective judgments of its value are informed by our respective unique sets of preferences, the judgments themselves are not commensurable on any single standard or criterion. Their value may not even be the same to *me* at one time as compared to a later time— there was a time, for example, when I did not appreciate Babe Ruth baseballs as much as I do now. Thus the valuations cannot be compared, and asking which is "objectively" worth more is incoherent.[7]

To the extent, then, that Smith has a labor theory of value, modern economics would judge that an important mistake.

Things have value based on how they are valued by individual agents, not based on anything inherently in them—whether labor or anything else. Yet Smith seems to waffle a bit on what exactly his theory of value is. He alternately suggests (1) that human labor is an objectively quantifiable, "universal" criterion, "never varying in its own value"; (2) that the value of labor is established by "the higgling and bargaining of the market"; and (3) that value relates to the "toil and trouble" that it would cost any valuing individual and thus might vary by individual.[8] Modern economists might be inclined to accept, with modifications, sense (2); they would be less happy with sense (3). They would reject altogether sense (1).[9]

I would point out, however, that Smith seems to emphasize the subjective nature of the relevant "labor": it relates to the particular individual who wants to acquire a thing. Smith writes that the "real price of everything, what every thing really costs *to the man who wants to acquire it*, is the toil and trouble of acquiring it"; moreover, what "every thing is really worth" to a man "is the toil and trouble which it can *save to himself*" (WN I.v.2; my emphasis).[10] So although Smith intends labor to be an objective criterion, it is indexed—and hence relative—to individuals. I would therefore call Smith's a *subjective-labor theory of value*.[11] I emphasize this interpretation because it fits better with Smith's reticence to predict what products will be produced in markets and what people will be willing to pay for them. Only individuals themselves can know how much of their labor they would save in buying something, and hence only individuals can know whether the price asked for something is worth it to them. Thus the goods that get produced in a market are in an important sense unplanned. The entrepreneur produces something at his own cost, and if the value of the good to individuals is greater than what it cost him to produce it—that is, if the "market price" is greater than the "real price"—then people will buy it, encouraging him to continue producing it. If it turns out that the reverse is the case, that the good's market price is below its real price to the entrepreneur, then the entrepreneur will suffer a loss, discouraging him from continuing to produce it. What drives market production, then, is the desires of the people acting in it, and their continuous attempts to satisfy those desires efficiently.[12]

Happiness and Tranquility

As we saw in Chapter 5, one principal constituent of happiness that Smith identifies in TMS is what he calls "tranquillity": "happiness consists in tranquillity and enjoyment. Without tranquillity there can be no enjoyment; and where there is perfect tranquillity there is scarce anything which is not capable of amusing" (TMS III.3.30). Many other passages contain similar sentiments; here is one more:

> Society and conversation, therefore, are the most powerful remedies for restoring the mind to its tranquillity, if, at any time, it has unfortunately lost it; as well as the best preservatives of that equal and happy temper, which is so necessary to self-satisfaction and enjoyment. (TMS I.i.4.10)

The attractiveness Smith sees of an easy contentment with one's situation is probably connected with the general affinity Smith has for Stoical philosophy. The ancient Stoics recommended the development of an *apatheia,* or a psychological equipoise independent of the vicissitudes of life. The strong self-discipline required to remain on an emotional even keel despite life's ups and downs impressed Smith deeply. He discovered it, for example, in the North American Indians, whose "passions, how furious and violent soever, are never permitted to disturb the serenity of [their] countenance or the composure of [their] conduct and behavior"; "Their magnanimity and self-command [. . .] are almost beyond the conception of Europeans" (TMS V.2.9). Smith clearly approved of this "self-command," as well as the even temper he thought it enabled, and part of his approval arose from his belief that this temper was connected with the tranquility he believed constituted happiness. In another striking passage, Smith writes that the "beggar, who suns himself by the side of the highway, possesses that security which kings are fighting for" (TMS IV.i.11).

If there is one thing that contemporary research indicates, however, about what states of mind enable, or even constitute, happiness, it is that being idle is not it. As Arthur Brooks has argued, for example, "work is an authentic source of happiness, and idleness—especially involuntary idleness—is a source of pure misery."[13] He continues:

"Very happy" people work more hours each week than those who are "pretty happy," who in turn work more hours than people who are "not too happy." Happy people work more in their free time than unhappy people. And having more hours to relax is not related to higher happiness. (Brooks 2008: 158)

To cite one other recent investigation, Charles Murray refers to what he calls the "Europe Syndrome," which is the general malaise effected by believing that "the purpose of life is to while away the time as pleasantly as possible."[14] Murray argues that the evidence suggests that such a conception of the point of human life is deadly to happiness: it may lead to pleasure, but not to happiness.[15]

Now, one might wish to draw some philosophical distinctions here. Idleness is not necessarily equivalent to tranquility; nor, perhaps, is Murray's "Europe Syndrome" equivalent to tranquility. Smith seemed to have in mind something deeper than mere wiling away the time. He wrote, for example,

The consciousness that it is the object of such favourable regards, is the source of that inward tranquillty and self-satisfaction with which it is naturally attended, as the suspicion of the contrary gives occasion to the torments of vice. What so great happiness as to be beloved, and to know that we deserve to be beloved? What so great misery as to be hated, and to know that we deserve to be hated? (TMS III.1.6)

Here Smith's suggestions seems to be that one's contentment rests on an awareness that one has achieved a level of virtue—that one is not just loved but also lovable; not just not hated, but not having done anything to deserve hate. That seems a more profound psychological state than simply contented pleasure, since the former seems attendant on a level of knowledge that does not usually accompany pleasurable contentment.

Smith comes closer to what current research has discovered when he claims that individuals' conduct is motivated "by their universal, continual, and uninterrupted effort to better their own condition" (WN II.iii.36). In WN, Smith goes so far as to say that this is "a desire which, though generally calm and dispassionate, comes with us from the womb, and never leaves us till we go into the grave"; he continues:

In the whole interval which separates those two moments,
there is scarce perhaps a single instant in which any man is so
perfectly and completely satisfied with his situation, as to be
without any wish of alternation or improvement of any kind.
(WN II.iii.28)

Smith may well be largely correct here—most people do seem
always to be always trying to better their conditions, according to
however each of them understands "better"—but the trouble is
that whether he is right about that or not, he does not connect
this industriousness with happiness. There is very little discussion of happiness at all in WN. When it does come up, Smith will
contrast it with "misery," which is not very helpful (see, for example, WN V.i.f.60); and in one place he suggests, consistent with
what he said in TMS, that it is closely connected to tranquility:
"No oppressive aristocracy has ever prevailed in the colonies.
Even they, however, would, in point of *happiness and tranquillity*,
gain considerably by a union with Great Britain" (WN V.iii.90;
my emphasis).

One might wish to find further fault with Smith for not explicitly investigating the nature of happiness in WN. If one goal of
economics as a discipline, after all, is investigating economic
ways by which people can become happy, then does the economist not owe us an indication of what his conception of happiness is? I think Smith's vague "bettering his own condition" is,
despite what one might initially think, a tremendous virtue of his
analysis, precisely because it does not presume to recommend or
adopt any single conception of the good. If you believe that
activity A betters your condition, then procuring means to
achieve A constitutes "wealth"—to you. Wealth, on this view, is
the accumulated means to achieve our ends, whatever they are.
By thus remaining neutral toward whether you ought or ought
not to be striving for A, Smith illustrates the value-neutrality that
would come to characterize the discipline of economics. Like
engineering, its principles are neither good nor bad in themselves; they are only descriptions of the way social institutions
work. Like wealth itself, economic knowledge is thus a tool—a
powerful tool—that can be used for good or bad ends. The agent
himself is responsible for the end toward which he puts that
knowledge (or his wealth); the economist is, and must be, content to uncover the ways of allowing more efficient procurement

of wealth for everyone, even while he knows that some people will misuse their wealth.

In a similar way, Smith's economic neutrality is moreover consistent with, and perhaps reflects, his argument that no centralized planner is competent to judge for others how or where they should expend their energies or capital. Recall:

> The statesman, who should attempt to direct private people in what manner they ought to employ their capitals, would not only load himself with a most unnecessary attention, but assume an authority which could safely be trusted, not only to no single person, but to no council or senate whatever, and which would nowhere be so dangerous as in the hands of a man who had folly and presumption enough to fancy himself fit to exercise it. (WN IV.ii.10)

This skepticism about the knowledge of statesmen (and political philosophers) is what leads Smith to recommend the devolution of government authority, leading, as this skepticism spread to ever more people in the British and American ambits, to the establishment of approximations of the Smithian limited government.

Committing the Great Mind Fallacy?

Finally, another objection one might raise to Smith is that he perhaps fell prey to his own Great Mind Fallacy (GMF).[16] In several places in WN, Smith endorses incursions into the market by third parties, often members of the government.[17] Even in the notable passage in which he recommends allowing the propagation of the "obvious and simple system of natural liberty" (WN IV.ix.51), Smith outlines three duties of government, the third and final of which is the "duty of erecting and maintaining certain publick works and certain publick institutions" (ibid.). The other two duties Smith names, protecting society from outside invasion and protecting citizens from invasions by one another, fall reasonably, one might suppose, within the boundaries set by a person advocating the limited government Smith describes. This limited government entails establishing an "exact administration of justice," which comprises, as we have seen, what Smith calls the three "sacred laws of justice"—protections of "the life and person of our neighbour," protections of our neighbor's "property and possessions," and protections of our neighbor's "personal rights, or what is due to him from the promises of others" (TMS II.ii.2.2). Smith's government thus protects life, liberty, property, and voluntary contracts, but little else. So why, then, would Smith suggest in WN that it should also undertake to provide some public goods? Do Smith's numerous recommended interventions into market exchanges constitute evidence that he himself is guilty of violating the GMF, believing he knows better than individuals where they should apply their capitals?

There are some uncharitable conclusions about Smith's argument one might draw, and at least one charitable conclusion. One of the uncharitable conclusions is that Smith is really a progressive, not a classical, liberal. That is, since he is interested in equity, equality, and the poor, although he understands that markets are necessary to produce wealth he nevertheless also understands that markets will have to be curbed to avoid excesses and managed in the service of higher ends. Several scholars today offer some version of this interpretation of Smith's political economy.[18] I count this is an uncharitable interpretation because it asks us to disregard too much of what Smith said—indeed to disregard what I have argued are some of the most central aspects of Smithian political economy, including the Economizer Argument, the Local Knowledge Argument, and the Invisible Hand Argument. Another uncharitable interpretation holds that Smith was simply confused. The person who articulated a careful delineation of the limited powers of government, of the benefits of free trade, of the dangers of "artificial" managing of economies, and of the dangers of businessmen joining hands with the state to use the latter's coercive powers to benefit themselves at the expense of the citizens: this person does not understand that those positions lead to various problems that he himself articulates. This too is a rather uncharitable description of Smith.

A better interpretation is that Smith articulated what he believed to be principles of good government, and the dangers to such government, based on his study of ancient and modern histories. He sees that his study suggests that people flourish best when wealth is growing, which itself takes place during periods when government enforces "justice" but does little else. He also sees, however, that human life is messier than many theorists would have it, and so sometimes exceptions to the principles are warranted for the benefit of the individuals or the local society involved. Hence his principles of limited government are defaults with presumptive authority. Exceptions to them are possible but must be argued for. Moreover, given the natural tendency of political, business, and academic leaders to overestimate their abilities to manage large-scale human social institutions, the burden of proof must be high. Proposed interventions in markets and in trade must be carefully scrutinized and their likely effects canvassed, and they must, before approval, demonstrate *both* that they will benefit the entire community (not only some portion of it at the expense of the rest) *and* that they cannot be provided by any private entrepreneurial initiative.[19] Those are difficult criteria to meet; indeed, many state incursions in Britain or America today would doubtless fail to meet them.

I suggest that the particular third-party market interventions Smith proposes are his considered guesses as to what might meet those two stringent criteria. We should expect that someone at the dawn of a new social age of commerce will get some of these guesses wrong; what is more astonishing is how many Smith gets right. But the point is that we can separate Smith's political principles and his criteria for marketplace intervention from his guesses as to what will meet those criteria. We can then accept the former while rejecting, or scrutinizing, the latter. For consider: It would not disprove the principles of the calculus if it turned out that some of Newton's calculations contained mistakes; it would not disprove the principles of evolutionary descent if it turned out that not all of the lineages Darwin outlined were correct; it would not disprove David Hume's theory of a standard of taste and of what constitutes a "true judge" of beauty if some of the particular judgments Hume makes are questionable or even false.[20] Similarly, it should not disprove Smith's principles of political economy if some of his hypothetical applications of those principles turn out to be questionable or even counterproductive.

Smith suggests in WN that the "publick institutions" and "publick works" that would meet his two criteria justifying state intervention in the market include institutions "for facilitating the commerce of the society, and those for promoting the instruction of the people" (WN V.i.c.2). Among the former Smith suggests "good roads, bridges, navigable canals, harbours, &c." (WN V.i.d.1). One might argue today that Smith's imagination about what markets could produce was insufficient to enable him to believe that they could produce all of those things privately, as private entrepreneurs have also produced institutions for promoting the instruction of the people as well. If so, that is an understandable limitation: few indeed could possibly have imagined the levels of wealth and the spectacular technological innovations that would characterize the next two centuries. More to the point here, however, I suggest that one should not take mistaken applications like these—if indeed they are mistakes—as evidence against the principles themselves. To discredit the principles, one should instead look to see what results from a *correct and consistent* application of them. Any principle can be misapplied; the dispositive question is whether, when applied correctly, they lead to the desired or predicted results. On this question, I suggest, Smith turns out to score very well.

Smithian Limited Government and Human Prosperity

During the nineteenth century, Smithian political economy— which included, as we have seen, recommendations of free markets; of free trade; of limited government intrusion into peaceful transactions; of state action confined for the most part to the protection of Smithian "justice," or protection of life, liberty, property, and voluntary contract; and of abolition of legal privileges for some classes of people over others[21]—began to influence policy in Great Britain, and from there to those places most affected by Great Britain, including especially the United States. Many other places, however, have not adopted Smithian recommendations. This affords us a remarkable opportunity to make a comparative assessment: How have the citizens of those places that more closely approximated Smithian recommendations fared in comparison to the citizens of those places that have not?

I close this chapter with a hint of what will come in the next by suggesting that this is one area where history has vindicated

Smith. In fact, the evidence is overwhelming. Here is one example. For several decades now, teams of economists have been assembling data from over 130 countries to compare the relative standard of living of their respective citizens. The now annually released *Economic Freedom of the World Index* (EFWI) rates countries on "economic freedom," which is a notably close approximation of Smithian political economy:

> Individuals have economic freedom when property they acquire without the use of force, fraud, or theft is protected from physical invasions by others and they are free to use, exchange, or give their property as long as their actions do not violate the identical rights of others. An index of economic freedom should measure the extent to which rightly acquired property is protected and individuals are engaged in voluntary transactions.[22]

The economists then compare those ratings against various measures of human welfare. The correlations are stark and revealing. The 2009 EFWI reports, for example, that the average per capita income of the countries in the top 25 percent of "economically free" is nearly ten times as high as the average per capita income of countries in the bottom 25 percent. Moreover, citizens in that top quartile score much higher on the United Nations Development Index than those in the bottom quartile, and citizens in the top quartile have an average life expectancy of over 20 years longer than that of the citizens in the bottom quartile. Indeed, Smithian "economic freedom" tracks positively with numerous measures of human well-being, including: per capita income, economic growth, life expectancy, low infant mortality, access to health care, access to potable water, levels of literacy, child nutrition, food production, percentage of gross domestic product dedicated to research, political stability, and peace. Correlation with a handful of these measures would be striking. But one does not need to be a statistician to see that correlation with this many—indeed, with nearly every measurable criterion by which people's well-being can be judged—is an astonishing confluence of evidence. The conclusion is that people fare much, much better in Smithian countries than in non-Smithian countries, and the more closely one's country approximates Smithian political economy, the better off one is likely to be.

That alone makes Smith's work among the most important in human history, regardless of whatever else he got right and regardless of whatever he might have gotten wrong. Still, one might want to know what else Smith got right. This brings us to Chapter 9.

Notes

[1] For discussion, see Blaug (1997), chapter 2; Hollander (1973), chapter 4; and Robertson and Taylor (1957). Rothbard (1995: vol. 1, 448) went so far as to write, "Adam Smith's doctrine on value was an unmitigated disaster."

[2] Marx would deepen the mysteriousness of this process by saying that labor "congeals" in an object to give it value. See, for example, Marx (1982 [1867]) pt I.

[3] For a discussion of the Austrian School's lineage and its development of the subjective theory of value, see Smith (1994), chapter 9. For discussions of how this school has influenced modern economic thought, see Vaughn (1998), esp. chapters 1–3.

[4] See Menger (2007 [1871]). For critical discussion of the PDMU, see Frankfurt (October 1987).

[5] Cited in Smith (1994), 283.

[6] See, respectively, St. Thomas (1948 [1266–73]), Question 78 on "Usury," and Cantillon (2001 [1755]), 15–17.

[7] See the classic accounts in Perry (2007 [1926]) and Mises (2010 [1940]). See also the essays in Kirzner (1986) and Frey and Morris (1993), and the discussions in Nozick (1981), 403–570 and Otteson (2006), chapter 4.

[8] For sense (1), see WN I.v.17 and I.v.7; for sense (2), see WN I.v.4; and for sense (3), see WN I.v.2.

[9] Rothbard (1995) argues that sense (1) is the only sense Smith has; on that basis he goes on to argue, rather implausibly, that Smith is therefore responsible for having derailed economic thought for approximately one hundred years.

[10] Cp. WN I.vii.5 and LJ, 495–6.

[11] This element of subjectivity would distinguish Smith's theory of value from that of Marx, protecting Smith from criticisms that have been leveled against Marx on this count. For an example of the standard interpretation of Smith's theory of value, see Raphael (1985), 63–4.

[12] See WN IV.ii.8–12.

[13] Brooks (2008), 156–7.

[14] Murray (2006), 83–4.

[15] See also Csikszentmihalyi (1990), Csikszentmihalyi (1997), Haidt (2006), and Layard (2005).

[16] See Chapter 6.

[17] See Kennedy (2005) for a discussion of some of Smith's recommended incursions.

[18] See, for example, Fleischacker (1999) and (2005).

[19] See WN V.i.c.1.

[20] See Hume's excellent "Of a Standard of Taste," in Hume (1987 [1741]).

[21] On this last point, see Peart and Levy (2005).

[22] Gwartney et al. (2009).

Chapter 9

What Smith Got Right

One way to assess a thinker who has had great influence in people's lives is to draw up something of a cost/benefit ledger of his contributions. At the end of Chapter 8, I suggested that Adam Smith's political-economic recommendations have led to vastly improved life prospects for those lucky enough to live in countries where they have been adopted. But there are other ways to assess a figure like Smith. One can ask, for example, what philosophical or scholarly contributions he made that have enduring significance. If Smith's labor theory of value and his conception of happiness as tranquility are places where Smith went wrong, where did Smith get it right? I believe Smith got much more right than he did wrong, justifying his place among the most important moral philosophers in the Western tradition. In this chapter, I indicate a handful of Smith's most important and enduring contributions.

Up First: Spontaneous Order

Smith suggested that complex systems of human social order are typically not centrally planned or designed from the top but, rather, generated unintentionally by the behaviors and decisions of agents acting within them. Large-scale human social orders are thus systems of unintentional order, or, as they are more often called today, "spontaneous order." That is one thing Smith seemed to have gotten right.

The spontaneous-order model that Smith developed has several elements. We have discussed them already, so I only summarize them here.

First, human beings have a *limited scope of knowledge*. They are most familiar with their own circumstances, including their own abilities, desires, and opportunities; they are somewhat less familiar with the circumstances of their closest family members and friends, still less of more distant family and friends, and so on, until we get to the vast majority of people in the world, whose circumstances they know not at all. If it is true that the person best positioned to make decisions about what a person should do to make himself happy is whoever has the most knowledge of the person in question, then, given the fact that each of us possesses only limited, "local" knowledge, it follows that the persons who should make these decisions are the persons in question themselves. This is what I have called Smith's Local Knowledge Argument.

The second feature is the role played by *cooperation and negotiation*. Because resources are scarce, and because people's desires frequently outstrip their abilities to procure on their own what they want, cooperation and negotiation are integral parts of human social life. In the area of morality, this means that people try to convince each other that their own behavior and judgments are correct and should be "sympathized" with, while in economic arenas this means people try to convince each other to exchange or contract with them on the terms or under the conditions they severally prefer. The people involved in these negotiations usually have no other purpose than to get the other person or persons involved to agree, exchange, or contract. They are setting precedents, however, which are the beginnings of habits that will shape their behavior in the future. Moreover, others might follow their example and begin to establish their own habits, protocols, and customs. Some such customs will get written into law, and some will come to be considered moral duty, perhaps even the will of God. These just are the systems of unintended order.

The third feature: *middle-way objectivity*. Although obedience to these systems of unintended order may be *considered* to be required by the will of God, the formation of the rules themselves does not require, and does not depend upon, any such transcendent sanction. The rules are instead developed by fallible human beings just trying to make their lives better. But the rules are not arbitrary. They enjoy a "middle-way" objectivity that is based on the joint, often tacit, agreement and beliefs of the people in question. Although they depend on the relevant historical tradition of individual decisions, no single person can create or change them on his own. They are self-enforced, often ruthlessly, even by people who would might be better off if different rules were in place. All this is usually without any official or explicit agreement to do so. So the rules are objective in that they exist and are followed, and that transgressions are punished; but they are not—at least not directly—dependent upon the will of God, on Platonic Forms, on Pure Reason, or on any other transcendent justification.

Fourth: *self-interest and the "familiarity principle."* Smith believed that human beings are driven by self-interest, but his notion of "self-interest" was broader than what is usually intended by that phrase today. It included the interests of those one cares about— one's family, one's friends, and so on. (Recall the first sentence of *The Theory of Moral Sentiments* (TMS): "How selfish soever man may be supposed, there are evidently some principles in his nature, which interest him in the fortune of others, and render their happiness necessary to him, though he derives nothing from it except the pleasure of seeing it."[1]) Those are *self*-interests because they are the person's alone, and because they can be indifferent to the interests of those outside the person's circles of concern. But that, Smith seemed to believe, is simply a fact of human nature: for the most part, we care more about ourselves than about anyone else, followed closely by our immediate family and best friends, followed in turn by other family and friends, then by acquaintances, and then last by strangers.[2] This descending level of benevolence toward others also, not coincidentally, correlates closely with our *familiarity* with them: the more familiar we are with someone, the more likely we are to be concerned about his welfare; and vice versa. I call this the *familiarity principle.* This principle also figures heavily into the way human social institutions are created and develop over time, not to mention the political and economic recommendations Smith went on to adopt.

Fifth: *general welfare and the "invisible hand."* Smith was under no illusion that people in their normal daily activities actually care about the general welfare. Luckily, however, people do not have to. The nature of the unintended systems of order suggests that they will tend to conduce to the benefit of everyone concerned regardless—at least in the long run. "In the long run" must be emphasized. There are numerous ways in which these systems of order can be derailed or corrupted, and hence not every system is actually or always beneficial. Smith seemed to think that the truly "natural" systems of order would in fact be beneficial, and, conversely, that if a system was not beneficial it was because it had suffered corruption and was hence no longer "natural."[3] Although he believed that some central aspects of human nature were fixed, he seemed to believe that moral philosophers could discern the fundamentals of nature and then base on them policies and institutions that would increase the chance of such creatures leading relatively happy and peaceful lives. So there could indeed be a *science* of jurisprudence whose ultimate goal is to enable people to flourish and be happy.

A Possible Problem. A brief digression on a contemporary objection raised to the Smithian market-model of spontaneous order will flesh out Smith's position.

Walter J. Schultz has recently argued that Smith's "Invisible Hand Claim," as Schultz calls it, fails. If we assume a population of "selfish" individuals who have only (1) desires they wish to satisfy and (2) rationality to discover means to their ends, Schultz argues that what ensues is not a spontaneously ordered system of conventions allowing individual uncoordinated actions to lead to socially beneficial results. To achieve *that* result it is necessary instead to supplement the initial scenario with several "moral" constraints. Specifically, Schultz argues that to get the Smithian optimistic result agents would have to recognize and abide by moral considerations like fair play and charity.[4] Schultz claims, however, that markets cannot spontaneously generate these necessary moral constraints, so he concludes that markets alone are insufficient to produce desirable overall social orders.

Many political theorists today criticize economics for assuming that people are amoral (even inhuman) rational utility maximizers. How, they ask, can economics accurately capture human social life if it systematically excludes from its models people who act from motives other than selfish ones or who act in ways that conflict with their own (narrowly conceived) interests?

A related objection raised to spontaneous-order theory is that human social life is an extremely complex Prisoner's Dilemma (PD), or perhaps an extremely complex series of PD problems. In the classic version of the PD, two criminals who made a pact with one another never to betray the other are faced with a prosecutor who offers each of them—separately—a deal whereby if he betrays the other by turning state's evidence against his accomplice, the betrayer will get a lighter sentence than the accomplice. The question or "dilemma" to each accused is, then, whether he should keep his promise or betray his accomplice. The standard treatment of the PD is that each of them should rationally betray, since, without perfect assurance that the other will also keep his word, he is better off trying to take the deal rather than risk being left holding the bag all by himself. Thus each prisoner rationally concludes he should confess, giving the prosecutor the best possible result, and each accused gets a result that neither wanted. Some argue that without an external, third-party agent to ensure that each person in the PD will keep his word, mutually less agreeable results inevitably ensue. Some then argue that this approximates human social life generally: without third-party enforcers—typically the state—people will not trust one another and will therefore betray one another, leading to socially suboptimal results. Without an externally provided motivation, the argument goes, purely selfish agents would inevitably take the mutually less beneficial options.[5] Thus the criticism is that the egoistic rational actors of "homo economicus" models of human behavior would create only inferior social orders. Therefore we should resist indulging only that aspect of our natures, and we should encourage our "moral"—here meaning *other-regarding*—motives as well.

In the mid-1980s, Robert Axelrod argued that PDs can be overcome spontaneously—that is, without the aid of external constraint—by repeated iterations of the exchanges in which the participants gain *reputations* or in which at least some participants can generate reliable intelligence on the basis of which to make reasonable judgments about people's likely courses of actions.[6] Axelrod argued that we face a great number of exchanges over the course of our lifetimes. After surveying many different rules of behavior that one might expect to facilitate cooperation, it turns out, Axelrod argued, that the simple "tit-for-tat" rule is the most successful. The tit-for-tat rule creates a system of punishments and rewards in the forms of noncooperation and cooperation that gives exchange partners, third-party observers, and even unknown others motivations to follow the rules that are discovered to be to mutual advantage.

Moreover, it generates intelligence about the individual actors—A cooperated last time; B did not; and so on—that actors could take into account when considering whether to attempt to cooperate with any given other actor. These two features—a system of punishments and rewards and reputations—acted, Axelrod argued, as powerful incentives to generate and then obey rules of behavior that facilitate exchanges in mutually or overall beneficial ways. Thus Axelrod's argument seemed to support Smithian optimism about invisible-hand generation of systems of unintended order.[7]

In some circumstances, however, Axelrod's tit-for-tat rule can break down, as for example in revenge-killings or family feuds: one bad act begets another bad act, which begets another, and so on, without obvious end. Thus Ken Binmore, for example, has argued that to get Axelrod's (or Smith's) results one would have to assume not the selfish economizer model of human nature but instead a model assuming agents who are *both* self-interested *and* altruistic.[8] Binmore claims that unless we assume some widespread natural altruistic motivation among agents, there will be no way (1) to prevent free riding, (2) to ensure that people will follow generally beneficial rules when following them would sacrifice or be prejudicial to their individual interests in particular cases, or (3) to provide sufficient certainty for everyone that others will not defect from the rules. Binmore's argument comports with Schultz's, which claims that market mechanisms require several additional, extra-market supplements to function in the way most free-market economists believe they can. Among these supplements are that agents have an inherent sense of right and wrong, a sense that corresponds to rules that actually would be conducive to widespread market cooperation, and that agents possess reliable knowledge about the motivations and characters of others with whom they would cooperate.

I think critics are right to suggest that a fuller conception of human nature is required for markets to be able to do what their proponents claim they can, including allocating moral, economic, and other resources in generally beneficial ways. But I suggest that a model that exploits the relevant features of human nature, including those that the "homo economicus" conception of human nature seems to leave out—principally a genuine altruism and a functioning desire and commitment, even if unconscious, to follow the socially beneficial rules—is in fact provided by the Smithian account of the market model. The part of Smith's model that satisfies this requirement is precisely the crown jewel of Smith's theory, the *desire for mutual sympathy of sentiments.* Recall that on the Smithian account human beings do not, in fact, want to satisfy only their own narrowly conceived ends: they are also interested in the "fortunes of others." Because, as Smith argues, human beings desire *mutual* sympathy of sentiments, they do in fact care what others think of their conduct. So Smith's market model is richer than the "homo economicus" model, and it may provide for exactly the kind of natural human motivation required to establish systems of spontaneous order that can in fact be generally beneficial. On Smith's model people do not care only about how they can get what they individually want; they also care about mutual sympathy of sentiments with others. The former guarantees that people will always form some kind of human society or other; the latter means they will tend to form systems of order that are mutually agreeable.

Thus the Smithian "market" version of a spontaneous-order model can, I submit, survive recent challenges to describe a creditable model explaining human behavior. Because Smith believes that his "market model" of spontaneous order applies to language (Chapter 2), to morality (Chapters 3 and 4), to economics (Chapter 6), and perhaps indeed to all human social orders (Chapter 7), I suggest that Smith's life work can be seen as an extended attempt to provide a *grand unification social theory,* applying it successively to various major aspects of human social life.

And the Smithian model has its proponents today. One principal twentieth-century economic proponent was Nobel Laureate economist Friedrich Hayek; another proponent today is Nobel Laureate economist Vernon Smith; and they are not alone.[9] A version of the Smithian model has its proponents in linguistics today as well: Rudi Keller, who subtitled one of his books *The Invisible Hand in Language Change;* Solikoko Mufwene, in whose most recent book "invisible hand" is one of the central organizing concepts; and Steven Pinker, one of the most influential linguists today, who also recognizes the spontaneous-order aspects of language.[10] The moral order Smith describes has not yet penetrated very far into contemporary moral philosophy, but even here a version of its model is, sometimes in conjunction with Hume's, becoming more widely discussed among moral theorists.[11] One central aspect of Smith's moral theory in particular—its reliance on the alleged universal human desire for "mutual sympathy of sentiments"—has received considerable recent empirical confirmation, a point to which we shall return momentarily.

Thus the Smithian market-model of spontaneous order is a powerful theory with wide-ranging implications that survive contemporary challenges and enjoys substantial contemporary attention and even support from a wide range of disciplines. It even anticipated, a century before Darwin, the twentieth-century calls for an ethical theory that is informed by a competent, empirically based understanding of human nature.[12] It would seem, then, that Smith might well have been on to something.[13]

Next Up: Sympathy of Sentiments

The Smithian answer to the problems of cooperation like those raised in the previous section suggests that the Smithian model is deserving of serious attention. Yet it has still more going for it: Modern researchers have discovered that we do, in fact, strongly desire mutual sympathy of sentiments. Reflecting various disciplinary perspectives, this apparently universal part of human nature has been called "conformism" to the thoughts and judgments of others (Boyd and Richerson 1990), an "exchange organ" that drives us to seek out social situations of reciprocal exchange (Barkow, Cosmides, and Tooby 1992), an "irrational" sacrificing of one's own interests (Frank 1988), a "sympathy knob" that can be dialed up or down by training and environment (Pinker 2003), "mirror neurons" and "synaesthesia" that unconsciously work to raise sentiments in one person similar to those that the person observes in others (Ramachandran 2000 and Ramachandran and Hubbard 2001), a "deep structure of fairness" embedded in our mental instincts (Binmore 2005), and a "mental organ" for imagining, and being concerned about, how "generalized others" see us (Harris 2006).[14]

Contemporary researchers have discovered that the knowledge that others would disapprove of us free riding, breaching contracts, reneging on promises, or making exceptions for ourselves from rules of behavior by which we expect others to live acts as a surprisingly effective disincentive to engage in such practices, and a strong incentive to pay our own way, to keep our promises, to honor our contracts, and to abide by general rules. The crucial point is that these are *natural* incentives—present, that is, without the aid of third-party intervention. Hence even if it is true that self-interest by itself is not enough to generate stable and beneficial social orders, it would not follow that the systems of unintended-order generated by Smithian invisible-hand mechanisms cannot allow people to spontaneously adopt behavioral norms that enable stable and beneficial social interaction. That would mean he was on to something indeed.

Third: Human Nature

In his book *A Conflict of Visions*, economist Thomas Sowell argued that much of the history of political and moral thought can be grouped under two competing "visions": the "constrained" and the "unconstrained." The exemplar Sowell selects for the "constrained" vision is none other than Adam Smith, whose position Sowell summarizes thus: "The moral limitations of man in general, and his egocentricity in particular, were neither lamented by Smith nor regarded as things to be changed. They were treated as inherent facts of life, the basic constraint in his vision" (2002: 12). Hence the name *constrained* vision: it holds that certain features of human nature, as well as the natural world, are fixed and unalterable, and thus that proper political economy must accept and adapt to those constraints. Along with Smith, Sowell includes in this category Edmund Burke, Friedrich Hayek, and the authors of *The Federalist Papers* (ibid., chapter 2). By contrast, the "unconstrained" vision holds that man's nature is malleable and can, with proper institutional attention and training, gradually improve over time so that vice can be reduced, even eliminated. The exemplar Sowell selects for the "unconstrained" vision is William Godwin, and he includes in this category Rousseau, Thomas Paine, and, more recently, Ronald Dworkin (ibid.).

As we have seen, Sowell is correct to place Smith under the "constrained" heading. Smith thought that certain aspects of human nature—like our basic motivations, our partiality for family and friends, our limited knowledge, and so on—were intractable, and thus a creditable political economy needed to recognize that. Smith also thought that certain aspects of our place in the world—like the fact that our desires outstrip our scarce resources—constitute constraints that also should inform our political economy.

I suggest that Smith is right here as well. Economics as a discipline today is veritably founded on assumptions that are largely those Smith suggested: human beings are "constrained" by tending to be self-interested, by tending to have limited benevolence, by tending to care more for those close to them than for those far away, and by their desires tending to outstrip their resources. That last feature is of fundamental importance. One standard definition of economics is that it is the study of how to allocate scarce resources that could be allocated in various competing ways.[15] Without scarcity of resources and without the existence of multiple competing uses to which those resources could be put, there would be no need for the discipline of economics; and if human beings did not have the abiding features of their nature that Smith suggested, economics would be nothing like what it is today.

As for whether human nature is malleable or not, the evidence here seems to be on Smith's side as well. To think otherwise is, for example, to deny evolutionary theory, which holds that human nature is the product of thousands and thousands of years of selection, and can be changed only very slowly— certainly not within a generation or two (or a hundred).[16] Thus Smith has Darwin on his side, a fact that both Darwin himself recognized,[17] and that contemporary evolutionary theorists recognize as well. Steven Pinker, for example, accepts Sowell's distinction between the "constrained" and "unconstrained" visions—though Pinker renames them "tragic" and "utopian," respectively—and he cites Adam Smith as he endorses the "constrained" or "tragic" vision.[18]

Another recent study provides corroboration of several aspects of Smith's conception of human nature. In her provocative recent book *No Two Alike*, Judith Rich Harris marshals evidence that supports Smith's conception of an impartial spectator and its role in adjudicating human behavior. Harris calls this perspective a "generalized other," and her description of the process that leads to the development of this perspective is astonishingly close to Smith's.[19] She also produces evidence of the generally beneficial effects of systems of spontaneous order, which she calls "self-organized systems," including in morality, where Harris argues that the systems develop according to our natural instinct to generate and pay attention to the perspective of the "generalized other."[20] Harris even cites Smith as a precursor to the most promising contemporary research about human status-seeking, commenting, "But Adam Smith, writing a century before Darwin, didn't know about evolution through natural selection. Or did he? He certainly seems to have had some of the relevant ideas."[21]

Fourth: Markets and Prosperity

In *The Wealth of Nations* (WN), Smith argued that if we observed the "obvious and simple system of natural liberty," in which all "systems of either preferences and restraints" were "completely taken away" and every man "left perfectly free to pursue his own interest his own way, and to bring both his industry and capital into competition with those of any other man, or order of men" (WN IV.ix.51), what would ensue is a "general plenty" and a "universal opulence," extending "itself to the lowest ranks of the people" (WN I.i.10). Was he right about that? Has the over two hundred years since Smith made those predictions vindicated or disproved him? Answer: vindication.

The evidence supporting this conclusion is voluminous. As economic history has improved over the last several decades, the data has accumulated and by now, I believe, justifies the judgment that Smithian political economy—including especially protections of private property, non-centrally planned market-based economies, and free trade—have been a greater benefit to humankind, including especially the poorest, than any other system of economic organization known. I shall here cite only a few bits of evidence, but I invite, even implore, the reader to investigate further.

Exhibit A is the *Economic Freedom of the World Index*, cited at the end of Chapter 8. Its accumulated data—all of which is downloadable for free at its website[22]—demonstrates that Smithian political economy, which the EFWI's economists call "economic freedom," is positively correlated with an extensive suite of measures of human welfare. EFWI's findings suggest that the more closely one's government approximates Smith's recommendations, the better off one is likely to be, and this holds *especially for the poor.* Exhibit B comes from economic historian Deidre McCloskey, who argues that despite the fact that "the world's population increased from 1800 to 2000 by a factor of about *six*," nevertheless "the amount of goods and services produced and consumed by the average person on the planet has *risen* since 1800 by a factor of about eight and a half"—as a result not of "social, humanitarian, and cosmopolitan forces," but rather "a result of liberal capitalism."[23] McCloskey goes on to corroborate and reinforce much of the evidence provided in the EFWI.[24] And Exhibit C comes from economists Maxim Pinkovskiy and Xavier Sala-i-Martin, who conclude, on the basis of their study of data from 191 countries, that Smithian political economy has reduced the worldwide poverty rate by fully 64 percent, rescuing some 700 million people from abject poverty since just 1970.[25]

Other evidence for Smithian political economy's beneficial effects, especially for the world's poor, abounds. Two World Bank economists recently looked at evidence from 92 countries over the last four decades regarding relative wealth and economic growth. Their conclusion: "a basic policy package of private property rights, fiscal discipline, macroeconomic stability, and openness to trade"—which the authors of the study identify as "pro-growth" policies—"on average increases the income of the poor to the same extent that it increases the income of the other households in society."[26] In other words, Smithian political economy makes *everyone* better off—with, in their words, no "trickle down" effect: "private property rights, stability, and openness contemporaneously create a good environment for poor households—and everyone else—to increase their production and income."[27] These authors investigated whether "government social spending, formal democratic institutions, primary school enrollment rates, and agricultural productivity" had positive effects on the prospects of the poor. Their conclusion:

> None of these variables has any robust relationship to either growth or to income share of the poor. Social spending as a share of total spending has a *negative* relationship to income share of the poor that is close to statistical significance.[28]

This is an astonishing finding. It suggests that not only were Smith's predictions largely correct, but also that the recommendations of those who disputed (and still dispute) Smith's recommendations—those who, that is, recommend that the government centrally redistribute income to enhance the prospects of the poor—are recommending policies that have a "negative" effect on the poor.

One final piece of evidence. Another telling way to compare places that have had Smithian economic institutions with those that have not is to look at the relative achievements of places like North Korea versus South Korea and China versus Hong Kong. In these cases we have people with similar cultures, languages, and other institutions, but who have adopted radically different economic institutions. The differences are stark. In North Korea, average per capita gross domestic product in 2008 was $1,800; in South Korea, it was $27,700.[29] In China, average per capita GDP in 2008 was $6,000; in Hong Kong, it was $43,800. These facts do not tell the entire story, of course, but they certainly are suggestive. And when they are combined with other evidence, the case in support of Smith's political economy recommendations becomes, I believe, compelling.

Notes

[1] Cp. This passage from Hume's *Treatise*: "For it must be confest, that however the circumstances of human nature may render an union necessary, and however those passions of lust and natural affection may seem to render it unavoidable; yet there are other particulars in our *natural temper*, and in our *outward circumstances*, which are very incommodious, and are even contrary to the requisite conjunction. Among the former, we may justly esteem our *selfishness* to be the most considerable. I am sensible, that, generally speaking, the representations of this quality have been carried on much too far [. . .]. So far from thinking, that men have no affection for anything beyond themselves, I am of opinion, that tho' it be rare to meet with one, who loves any single person better than himself; yet 'tis as rare to meet with one, in whom all the kind affections, taken together, do not over-balance the selfish" (Hume 2000 [1739–40], 3.2.2; emphasis in the original).

[2] There are exceptions to these generalities, of course—sometimes we can care about others' interests even more than our own, for example—but the generalization depends on overall trends.

[3] The term "natural" here has lots of possible connotations, but Smith thought that most common way for a "natural" system to become corrupted, and thus *un*natural, was by third-party, usually coercive, interposition.

[4] Schultz (2001), 105.

[5] See Danielson (May 14, 2002).

[6] This is Hayek's point in his discussions of "reputation"; see Hayek (1980). See also Bradley (2005) and Klein (1997).

[7] See Axelrod (1984), (October 1985), and (1997).

[8] See Binmore (1994). More recently, Binmore (2005) argues for an agent with an instinctive sense of "fairness."

[9] See Hayek (1945), Hayek (1960), and Smith (2002); see also Macleod (2007).

[10] See Keller (1995), Mufwene (2008), and Pinker (1994). See also Kenneally (2007).

[11] See, for example, Baier (1991), Graham (2004), Griswold (1999), Harman (1977), Hocutt (2000), Joyce (2006), and Rubin (2002).

[12] For a contemporary example of an appeal to moral philosophers to ground their theories in empirical evidence, see Wilson (1999), chapter 11. See also Evensky (2005).

[13] For other recent uses of spontaneous-order theory from a variety of fields, see Harris (2006), Heath (Summer 2007), Kauffman (1993), Shermer (2009), Sunstein (2008b), and Vanderbilt (2008).

[14] See also Alexander (1987), Ridley (1998), Singer (1981), Wilson (1997), Wilson (1998), and Wilson (2004).

[15] Lionel Robbins definition, quoted in Sowell (2007), 2.

[16] See Cochran and Harpending (2009).

[17] In his *Descent of Man*, Darwin cites Smith approvingly, referring to Smith's "striking" argument. See Darwin (1981 [1871]), 81.

[18] Pinker (2002), chapter 16.

[19] Harris (2006), chapter 9.

[20] Ibid., esp. 233–7.

[21] Ibid., 238. See also Ridley (1998), on which Harris draws and which itself explicitly draws on Smith.

[22] Available here: http://www.freetheworld.com/.

[23] McCloskey (2006), 17–18; emphasis in the original. See also Bethel (1998), Maddison (2007a) and (2007b), and Pipes (1999).

[24] Ibid., "Apology."

[25] Pinkovskiy and Sala-i-Martin (2009).

[26] Dollar and Kraay (September 2002), 218–19.

[27] Ibid.

[28] Dollar and Kraay (2002), 8–9; emphasis supplied.

[29] These figures are taken from the CIA's *World Fact Book*. See also Higgs (2004), chapters 21 and 22.

Epilogue
Smith: Conservative or Libertarian?

It is hard to classify Adam Smith politically, since he seems to embody elements of today's notion of "liberal" and "conservative," as well as "libertarian."[1] He was certainly no anarchist, and, since he apparently did not subscribe to a theory of natural rights, he was no Lockean either. He believed history demonstrated the necessity of a government defending private property and interfering only little in people's economic affairs. Yet he was pragmatic about his principles: they were defaults that could, in exigencies, be violated. He was thus no principled purist, which probably disqualifies him as a libertarian, at least of the Nozickean or Radian type. He was instead an old-fashioned liberal: favoring individual liberty, endorsing state institutions to protect this liberty, and, where they conflicted, favoring the individual over the state as a default. But he was also a skeptical empiricist. He favored free trade, free markets, and a government robust but limited to the enforcement of a few central tasks not because they comported with *a priori* principles but because they seemed to work. He tended toward optimism about the future, and about what lay ahead for humanity if much of the apparatus of government meddling was dismantled; yet by the same token he was not optimistic that truly free trade—or, probably, truly free markets—would ever be fully realized, because doing so would make it too difficult for grasping politicians to extend their power and for corrupt businessmen to profit at others' expense.

Smith was also a champion of the poor. He was interested, as an empirical scientist should be, to discover how economies work and the way human psychology works; yet he was also interested, as a moral philosopher should be, to recommend political and economic strategies to minimize suffering and to maximize flourishing. He believed that human beings of all social classes and races shared a rough equality in abilities and motivations—a radical notion at the time.[2] And he repeatedly expressed his concern not for the rich and privileged but for the lower classes, the poor, and workers. He recognized that businessmen would often seek special privileges to increase their profits or decrease competition, despite the fact that these privileges would invariably make the common man worse off.[3] He thus strongly opposed partnerships between business and government. And he worried about the effects on workers of extreme division of labor. What would happen to them, he asked, if they spent all their hours repeating simple operations, without ever exercising their higher faculties?[4] To alleviate the potentially mind-numbing effects of repetitive simple operations, he suggested partially subsidized primary schooling. This constitutes a departure from his otherwise non-interventionist stance, but he seemed to think the greater good might justify it.[5]

Smith's concern for the poor leads some commentators to suggest that he must have been a proto-"progressive" liberal, since, as some believe, only progressive liberals care about the poor. Samuel Fleischacker, for example, argues that Smith's concern for the poor is one reason to see him as "left-leaning" rather than "right-leaning."[6] Concern for the poor is, however, hardly the exclusive provenance of the political left. And Smith's strong arguments in favor of decentralization of power, competition, and free markets would seem to put him rather on the right of today's political spectrum than on the left.

Russell Kirk, to take a prominent twentieth-century example, identifies Smith as one of the forefathers—along with Edmund Burke—of the "conservative" tradition with which he aligns himself.[7] Nobel Laureate economist Friedrich Hayek, on the other hand, also claims Smith, along with Hume and Burke, as his own intellectual forebear, yet Hayek rejects the label "conservative" and calls himself a "liberal" instead.[8] Nobel Laureate economist Milton Friedman, who also considered himself a student and follower of Smith, similarly rejected the label "conservative" and called himself a "liberal."[9]

I would instead call Smith a *classical liberal*. Favoring private property, free markets, and free trade; trusting individual people to direct their own affairs rather than centralized government officials; believing that no political institutions will eradicate human failings and that no class of human beings is inherently better, more virtuous, or worthier than any other; recommending local control and private enterprise wherever possible: these are the central defining characteristics of the "liberalism" that arose largely in Britain in the eighteenth and nineteenth centuries.[10] The qualifier "classical" serves not to make this liberalism a mere historical artifact, but rather to signal that it is part of a tradition that is distinct from much contemporary liberalism. Perhaps "skeptical, pragmatic, empirical libertarian" is a more accurate description of Smith's political economy, but that is a bit cumbersome.

Yet let us not quarrel about labels. Wherever he falls on the map of political-economic positions, Smith constructed a plausible and powerful model for understanding human social institutions, and he had the greatness of soul to sincerely wish to put it to use to benefit mankind. He was thus a grand unification theorist of human sociality, and one of the world's great humanitarians. In his own mind those two activities combined into one endeavor: "moral philosophy." Perhaps, then, "moral philosopher"—which is, after all, what Smith called himself—is the most fitting label.

Notes

[1] Brubaker (2006) claims that Smith was "neither a conservative nor a libertarian," while Griswold (1999) claims that it is "impossible to see Smith as either 'conservative' or 'liberal,' 'right' or 'left,' in the contemporary American sense of these terms" (295 n64). McLean (2006), for his part, calls Smith a "radical egalitarian," while Kennedy (2005) and (2008) offers a mixed Smith who subscribes neither to laissez-faire nor to contemporary European-style welfare-statism.

[2] WN I.ii.4–5. See Peart and Levy (2005).

[3] "People of the same trade seldom meet together, even for merriment and diversion, but the conversation ends in a conspiracy against the publick, or in some contrivance to raise prices" (WN I.x.c.27). See also WN I.vii.13.

[4] WN V.i.f.50.

[5] More specifically, he suggested that public primary schooling might satisfy his two criteria justifying government provision of a public good—namely, that they benefit everyone, and that no private person or group could profit from providing them in the market (see WN V.i.c.1). Note that this intrusion on the free market that

Smith endorses is quite a weak one: *partially* subsidized (less than half, he says) *primary* schooling (not high school, let alone college) (WN V.i.f.55). He suggests that teaching people to "read, write, and account" is basically all they need—something that can be accomplished with only a few years of primary schooling (see, e.g., WN V.i.f.16). And yet even here Smith recommends creating as much competition and local authority in education as possible (see, e.g., WN V.i.f.4 and V.i.f.12)

[6] See Fleischacker (2005), §§49 and 51. Fleischacker elsewhere claims that "Those who construe freedom as noninterference tend to promote hands-off government policies to a degree that can be breathtakingly callous to the poor" (1999: 3); since Smith was not "breathtakingly callous toward the poor," Fleischacker concludes he was therefore no advocate of limited government. See also Rothschild (2001).

[7] See, for example, Kirk (1954), chapter 1 and (1986 [1953]), chapter 1.

[8] See, for example, Hayek (1960), chapter 4 and Postscript.

[9] See, for example, Friedman (2002 [1962]), Introduction.

[10] See Berlin (2008 [1969]).

Bibliography

Primary Sources

Aristotle. 2000 (*ca.* 330 BC). *Nicomachean Ethics.* Roger Crisp, ed. Cambridge: Cambridge University Press.

Bastiat, Frédéric. 1995 (1850). "What Is Seen and What Is Not Seen." In *Selected Essays on Political Economy,* ed. George B. de Huszar. Irvington-on-Hudson: Foundation for Economic Education, 1–50.

Cantillon, Richard. 2001 (1755). *Essay on the Nature of Commerce in General.* New Brunswick, NJ: Transaction.

Darwin, Charles. 1981 (1871). *The Descent of Man, and Selection in Relation to Sex.* Princeton: Princeton University Press.

Ferguson, Adam. 1995 (1767). *An Essay on the History of civil Society.* Fania Oz-Salzberger, ed. Cambridge: Cambridge University Press.

Hume, David. 1975 (1748). *An Enquiry Concerning Human Understanding.* L. A. Selby-Bigge and P. H. Nidditch, eds. New York: Oxford University Press.

Hume, David. 1987 (1741). "Of a Standard of Taste." In Eugene F. Miller, ed., *Essays Moral Political and Literary.* Indianapolis: Liberty Fund, 226–49.

Hume, David. 2000 (1739–40). *A Treatise of Human Nature.* David Fate Norton and Mary J. Norton, eds. Oxford: Oxford University Press.

Hume, David. 2006 (1751). *An Enquiry Concerning the Principles of Morals.* Tom L. Beauchamp, ed. Oxford: Oxford University Press.

Malthus, Thomas R. 1986. *The Works of Thomas Robert Malthus,* 8 vols. E. A Wrigley and D. Souden, eds. London: William Pickering.

Mandeville, Bernard. 1988 (1714). *The Fable of the Bees: or Private Vices, Publick Benefits,* 2 vols. F. B. Kaye, ed. Indianapolis: Liberty Fund.

Marx, Karl. 1982 (1867). *Capital,* vol. 1. New York: Penguin Classics.

Menger, Carl. 2007 (1871). *Principles of Economics.* Auburn, AL: Ludwig von Mises Institute.

Newton, Isaac. 1713 (1687). *Philosophiae Naturalis Principia Mathematica,* rev. 2nd. ed.

Plato. 1992 (*ca.* 380 BC). *Republic.* G. M. A. Grube, trans. with rev. from C. D. C. Reeve. Indianapolis: Hackett, 1992.

Reid, Thomas. 1991 (1788). *Essays on the Powers of Man.* In *British Moralists 1650–1800,* vol. II, D. D. Raphael, ed. Indianapolis: Hackett.

Rousseau, Jean-Jacques. 1987 (1754). *Discourse on the Origins of Inequality.* In *Jean-Jacques Rousseau: The Basic Political Writings,* Donald A. Cress, ed. Indianapolis: Hackett, 25–81.

Rousseau, Jean-Jacques. 2003 (1754). "Luxury, Commerce, and the Arts." In *Commerce, Culture, and Liberty: Readings on Capitalism before Adam Smith,* Henry C. Clark, ed. Indianapolis: Liberty Fund.

Thomas, St. of Aquinas. 1948 (1266–73). *Summa Theologica.* New York: Benzinger Bros.

Secondary Sources

Adair, Douglass. 1998. "Fame and the Founding Fathers." In *Fame and the Founding Fathers: Essays by Douglass Adair,* Trevor Colbourn, ed. Indianapolis: Liberty Fund, 3–36.

Alexander, Richard. 1987. *The Biology of Moral Systems.* Hawthorne, NY: Aldine de Gruyter.

Alvey, James. 2003. *Adam Smith: Optimist or Pessimist? A New Problem Concerning the Teleological Basis of Commercial Society.* Burlington, VT: Ashgate.

Aspromourgos, Tony. 2009. *The Science of Wealth: Adam Smith and the Framing of Political Economy.* London: Routledge.

Axelrod, Robert. 1984. *The Evolution of Cooperation.* New York: Basic Books.

Axelrod, Robert. 1997. *The Complexity of Cooperation: Agent-Based Models of Competition and Collaboration.* Princeton: Princeton University Press.

Axelrod, Robert and Robert O. Keohane. October 1985. "Achieving Cooperation under Anarchy: Strategies and Institutions." *World Politics* 37, 1: 226–54.

Baier, Annette C. 1991. *A Progress of Sentiments: Reflections on Hume's "Treatise."* Cambridge: Harvard University Press.

Barkow, Jerome H., Leda Cosmides, and John Tooby. 1992. *The Adapted Mind: Evolutionary Psychology and the Generation of Culture.* New York: Oxford.

Berlin, Isaiah. 2008 (1969). "Two Concepts of Liberty." In *Isaiah Berlin: Liberty,* Henry Hardy, ed. New York: Oxford University Press, 166–217.

Berry, Christopher. 1974. "Adam Smith's *Considerations* on Language." *Journal of the History of Ideas* 35: 130–38.

Berry, Christopher. 1997. *Social Theory of the Scottish Enlightenment.* Edinburgh: Edinburgh University Press.

Bethel, Tom. 1998. *The Noblest Triumph: Property and Prosperity through the Ages.* New York: St. Martin's.

Binmore, Ken. 1994. *Game Theory and the Social Contract, Vol. I: Playing Fair.* Cambridge, MA: MIT Press.

Binmore, Ken. 2005. *Natural Justice.* Oxford: Oxford University Press.

Blaug, Mark. 1997. *Economic Theory in Retrospect,* 5th ed. Cambridge: Cambridge University Press.

Boyd, Robert and Peter Richerson. 1990. "Culture and Cooperation." In *Beyond Self-Interest,* Jane J. Mansbridge, ed. Chicago: University of Chicago Press, 111–32.

Bradley, Robert L. Jr. 1 April 2005. "Getting to Know You: Reputation and trust in a Two-Person Economic Exchange." *Science* 308, 5718: 78–83.

Broadie, Alexander. 2001. *The Scottish Enlightenment.* Edinburgh: Birlinn.

Brooks, Arthur. 2008. *Gross National Happiness: Why Happiness Matters for America—and How We Can Get More of It.* New York: Basic Books.

Brubaker, Lauren. 2006. "Why Adam Smith Is Neither a Conservative Nor a Libertarian." *Adam Smith Review,* 2: 197–202.

Camerer, Colin F. March 2007. "Using Neuroeconomics to Make Economic Predictions." *Economic Journal* 117: C26–C42

Campbell, T. D. 1971. *Adam Smith's Science of Morals.* London: Allen and Unwin.

Cannan, Edwin ed. 1896. *Lectures on Justice, Police, Revenue and Arms, delivered in the University of Glasgow by Adam Smith.* Oxford: Oxford University Press.

Cochran, Gregory and Henry Harpending. 2009. *The 10,000 Year Explosion: How Civilization Accelerated Human Evolution.* New York: Basic Books.

Cropsey, Joseph. 1957. *Polity and Economy: An Interpretation of the Principles of Adam Smith.* Martinus Nijhoff: The Hague.

Csikszentmihalyi, Mihaly. 1990. *Flow: The Psychology of Optimal Experience.* New York: Harper & Row.

Csikszentmihalyi, Mihaly. 1997. *Finding Flow.* New York: Basic Books.

Danielson, Peter. May 14, 2002. "Competition Among Cooperators: Altruism and Reciprocity." *Proceedings of the National Academy of Science* 99, 3: 7237–7242.

De Waal, Franz. 2007. *Chimpanzee Politics: Power and Sex Among Apes,* 25th anniversary ed. Baltimore: Johns Hopkins Press.

Denis, Andy. 2005. "The Invisible Hand of God in Adam Smith." *Research in the History of Economic Thought and Methodology,* 23, A: 1–32.

Dollar, David and Aart Kraay. 2002. "Growth Is Good for the Poor." Washington, DC: World Bank.

Dollar, David and Aart Kraay. September 2002. "Growth Is Good for the Poor." *Journal of Economic Development* 7, 3: 195–225.

Evensky, Jerry. 2005. *Adam Smith's Moral Philosophy: A Historical and Contemporary Perspective on Markets, Law, Ethics, and Culture.* Cambridge: Cambridge University Press.

Fleischacker, Samuel. 1999. *A Third Concept of Liberty: Judgment and Freedom in Kant and Adam Smith.* Princeton: Princeton University Press.

Fleischacker, Samuel. October 2002. "Adam Smith's Reception among the Founders, 1776–1790." *William and Mary Quarterly,* 3rd Series, 59, no. 4: 897–924.

Fleischacker, Samuel. 2005. *On Adam Smith's "Wealth of Nations": A Philosophical Companion.* Princeton: Princeton University Press.

Frank, Richard H. 1988. *Passions within Reason.* New York: Norton.

Frankfurt, Harry G. October 1987. "Equality as a Moral Ideal." *Ethics* 98, 1: 21–43.

Friedman, Milton. 2002 (1962). *Capitalism and Freedom.* Chicago: University of Chicago Press.

Frey, R. G. and Christopher W. Morris, eds. 1993. *Value, Welfare, and Morality.* Cambridge: Cambridge University Press.

Göçmen, Doğan. 2009. *The Adam Smith Problem: Reconciling Human Nature and Society in "The Theory of Moral Sentiments" and "Wealth of Nations."* London and New York: Tauris Academic Studies.

Graham, Gordon. 2004. *Eight Theories of Ethics.* London and New York: Routledge.

Griswold Jr., Charles L. 1999. *Adam Smith and the Virtues of Enlightenment.* Cambridge: Cambridge University Press.

Gwartney, James and Robert Lawson 2009. *Economic Freedom of the World Index.* Vancouver: Fraser Institute.

Haakonssen, Knud. 1981. *The Science of a Legislator: The Natural Jurisprudence of David Hume and Adam Smith.* Cambridge: Cambridge University Press.

Haakonssen, Knud. 2006. "Introduction: The Coherence of Smith's Thought." *The Cambridge Companion to Adam Smith,* Knud Haakonssen, ed. Cambridge: Cambridge University Press, 1–21.

Haidt, Jonathan. 2006. *The Happiness Hypothesis: Finding Modern Truth in Ancient Wisdom.* New York: Basic Books.

Handbook of Official Rules for Major League Baseball. Available here: http://mlb.mlb.com/mlb/official_info/official_rules/foreword. jsp.

Hanley, Ryan Patrick. 2009. *Adam Smith and the Character of Virtue.* Cambridge: Cambridge University Press.

Harman, Gilbert. 1977. *The Nature of Rationality: An Introduction to Ethics.* Oxford: Oxford University Press.

Harris, Judith Rich. 2006. *No Two Alike: Human Nature and Human Individuality.* New York: W. W. Norton.

Hayek, Friedrich A. 1960. *The Constitution of Liberty.* Chicago: University of Chicago Press.

Hayek, Friedrich A. 1980 (1945). "The Use of Knowledge in Society." Reprinted in his *Individualism and Economic Order.* Chicago: University of Chicago Press, 77–91.

Heath, Will C. Summer 2007. "Hayek Revisited: Planning, Diversity, and the Vox Populi." *The Independent Review* XII, 1: 47–70.

Higgs, Robert. 2004. *Against Leviathan: Government Power and a Free Society.* Oakland, CA: Independent Institute.

Hocutt, Max. 2000. *Grounded Ethics: The Empirical Bases of Normative Judgments.* New Brunswick: Transaction.

Hocutt, Max. Fall 2003. "Compassion without Charity, Freedom without Liberty: The Political Fantasies of Jean-Jacques Rousseau." *The Independent Review* 8, 2: 165–91.

Hollander, Samuel. 1973. *The Economics of Adam Smith.* Toronto: University of Toronto.

Hull, David. 1998. *Science as a Process.* Chicago: University of Chicago Press.

Joyce, Richard. 2006. *The Evolution of Morality.* Cambridge: MIT Press.

Kahneman, Daniel and Amos Tversky, eds. 2000. *Choices, Values, and Frames.* Cambridge: Cambridge University Press.

Kauffman, Stuart A. 1993. *The Origins of Order: Self-Organization and Selection in Evolution.* New York: Oxford University Press.

Keller, Rudi. 1995. *On Language Change: The Invisible Hand in Language.* London: Routledge.

Kenneally, Christine. 2007. *The First Word: The Search for the Origins of Language.* New York: Viking Penguin.

Kennedy, Gavin. 2005. *Adam Smith's Lost Legacy.* Palgrave Macmillan.

Kennedy, Gavin. 2008. *Adam Smith.* Palgrave Macmillan.

Kirk, Russell. 1954. *A Program for Conservatives.* Chicago: Regnery.

Kirk, Russell. 1986 (1953). *The Conservative Mind: From Burke to Eliot,* 7th ed. Washington, DC: Regnery.

Kirzner, Israel M., ed. 1986. *Subjectivism, Intelligibility, and Economic Understanding.* New York: New York University Press.

Kleer, Richard A. 1995. "Final Causes in Adam Smith's *Theory of Moral Sentiments.*" *Journal of the History of Philosophy* 33 (April): 275–300.

Klein, Daniel B., ed. 1997. *Reputation: Studies in the Voluntary Elicitation of Good Conduct.* Ann Arbor: University of Michigan Press.

Kuhn, Thomas S. 1977. "Objectivity, Value Judgment, and Theory Choice." In his *The Essential Tension: Selected Studies in Scientific Tradition and Change.* Chicago: University of Chicago Press, 320–39.

Kuhn, Thomas S. 1996 (1962). *The Structure of Scientific Revolutions,* 3rd ed. Chicago: University of Chicago Press.

Layard, Richard. 2005. *Happiness: Lessons from a New Science.* New York: Penguin.

Macfarlane, Alan. 2000. *The Riddle of the Modern World: Of Liberty, Wealth, and Equality.* New York: St. Martin's.

Macleod, Alistair M. 2007. "Invisible Hand Arguments: Milton Friedman and Adam Smith." *The Journal of Scottish Philosophy* 5, 2: 103–117.

Maddison, Angus. 2007a. *Contours of the World Economy, 1–2030AD: Essays in Macro-Economic History.* Oxford: Oxford University Press.

Maddison, Angus. 2007b. *The World Economy: A Millennial Perspective.* Washington, DC: Organization for Economic Cooperation and Development.

McCloskey, Deirdre M. 2006. *The Bourgeois Virtues: Ethics for an Age of Commerce.* Chicago: University of Chicago Press.

McLean, Iain. 2006. *Adam Smith: Radical and Egalitarian: An Interpretation for the 21st Century.* Edinburgh: Edinburgh University Press.

Minowitz, Peter. 1993. *Profits, Priests, and Princes.* Stanford: Stanford University Press.

Mises, Ludwig von. 2010 (1940). *Human Action.* Indianapolis: Liberty Fund.

Montes, Leonidas. 2004. *Adam Smith in Context: A Critical Reassessment of some Central Components of His Thought.* Palgrave Macmillan.

Mufwene, Salikoko S. 2008. *Language Evolution: Contract, Competition, and Change.* London: Continuum.

Muller, Jerry Z. 1993. *Adam Smith in His Time and Ours: Designing the Decent Society.* New York: Free Press.

Murray, Charles. 2006. *In Our Hands: A Plan to Replace the Welfare State.* Washington, DC: American Enterprise Institute for Public Policy Research.

New York Times. November 19, 1996. "Paradise Lost: Biosphere Retooled as Atmospheric Nightmare."

New York Times. September 9, 2003. "Columbia University Ends Its Association with Biosphere 2."

Nieli, Russell. 1986. "Spheres of Intimacy and the Adam Smith Problem." *Journal of the History of Ideas* 47, 4: 611–24.

Nozick, Robert. 1974. *Anarchy, State, and Utopia.* New York: Basic Books.

Nozick, Robert. 1981. *Philosophical Explanations.* Cambridge: Belknap.

Oncken, August. 1987. "The Consistency of Adam Smith." *Economic Journal of London* vii: 443–50.

Oslington, Paul, ed. Forthcoming. *Adam Smith as Theologian.* London: Routledge.

Otteson, James R. January 2000. "The Recurring 'Adam Smith Problem.'" *History of Philosophy Quarterly* 17, 1: 51–74.

Otteson, James R. January 2002a. "Adam Smith's First Market: The Development of Language." *History of Philosophy Quarterly* 19, 1: 65–86.

Otteson, James R. 2002b. *Adam Smith's Marketplace of Life.* Cambridge: Cambridge University Press.

Otteson, James R. 2006. *Actual Ethics.* Cambridge: Cambridge University Press.

Otteson, James R. 2010a. "Adam Smith and the Great Mind Fallacy." *Social Philosophy and Policy* 27, 1: 276–304.

Otteson, James R. 2010b. "The Scottish Enlightenment and the Tragedy of Human Happiness." In *On Happiness*, Kelly Clark, ed. Beijing: The World Knowledge Press.

Paganelli, Maria Pia. 2008. "The Adam Smith Problem in Reverse: Self-Interest in *The Wealth of Nations* and *The Theory of Moral Sentiments*." *History of Political Economy* 40, 2: 365–382.

Peart, Sandra J. and David M. Levy. 2005. *The "Vanity of the Philosopher": From Equality to Hierarchy in Post-Classical Economics.* Ann Arbor: University of Michigan Press.

Perry, Ralph Barton. 2007 (1926). *General Theory of Value.* New York: Grierson Press.

Pinker, Steven. 1994. *The Language Instinct.* New York: William Morrow.

Pinker, Steven. 2003. *The Blank Slate: The Modern Denial of Human Nature.* New York: Penguin.

Pinkovskiy, Maxim and Xavier Sala-i-Martin. 2009. "Parametric Estimations of the World Distribution of Income." Cambridge, MA: National Bureau of Economic Research.

Pipes, Richard. 1999. *Property and Freedom.* New York: Vintage.

Popper, Karl. 2000 (1963). *Conjectures and Refutations: The Growth of Scientific Knowledge.* New York: Routledge.

Rae, John. 1895. *Life of Adam Smith.* London: Macmillan.

Ramachandran, V. S. June 1, 2000. "Mirror Neurons and Imitation Learning as the Driving Force behind 'the Great Leap Forward' in Human Evolution." *Edge* 69.

Ramachandran, V. S. and E. M. Hubbard. 2001. "Synaesthesia—A Window into Perception, Thought and Language." *Journal of Consciousness Studies* 8, 12: 3–34.

Raphael, D. D. 1985. *Adam Smith.* Oxford: Oxford University Press.

Raphael, D. D. 2007. *The Impartial Spectator: Adam Smith's Moral Philosophy.* Oxford: Oxford University Press.

Rashid, Salim. 1998. *The Myth of Adam Smith.* Cheltenham: Edward Edgar.

Rasmussen, Dennis. 2008. *The Promise and Problems of Commercial Society: Adam Smith's Response to Rousseau.* University Park, PA: Pennsylvania State University Press.

Ridley, Matt. 1998. *The Origins of Virtue: Human Instincts and the Evolution of Cooperation.* New York: Penguin.

Robbins, Lionel. 1952. *The Theory of Economic Policy.* London: Macmillan.

Robertson, H. M. and W. L. Taylor. June 1957. "Adam Smith's Approach to the Theory of Value." *Economic Journal*: 182–98

Ross, Ian S. 1995. *The Life of Adam Smith.* Oxford: Oxford University Press.

Rothbard, Murray. 1995. *An Austrian Perspective on the History of Economic Thought*, vol. I. Cheltenham: Edward Elgar.

Rothschild, Emma. 2001. *Economic Sentiments: Adam Smith, Condorcet, and the Enlightenment*. Cambridge: Harvard University Press.

Rubin, Paul H. 2002. *Darwinian Politics: The Evolutionary Origin of Freedom*. New Brunswick: Rutgers University Press.

Schelling, Thomas C. 1978. *Micromotives and Macrobehavior*. New York: Norton.

Schliesser, Eric. 2002. "Adam Smith's Theoretical Endorsement of Deception." *Adam Smith Review* 2: 209–14.

Schliesser, Eric. 2005. "Realism in the Face of Scientific Revolutions: Adam Smith on Newton's 'Proof' of Copernicanism." *British Journal for the History of Philosophy* 13, 4: 697–732.

Schultz, Walter J. 2001. *The Moral Conditions of Economic Efficiency*. Cambridge: Cambridge University Press.

Schumpeter, Joseph A. 1975 (1942). *Capitalism, Socialism and Democracy*. New York: Harper and Row.

Searle, John. 1997. *The Construction of Social Reality*. New York: Free Press.

Shermer, Michael. 2009. *The Mind of the Market: How Biology and Psychology Shape Our Economic Lives*. New York: Holt Publishing.

Singer, Peter. 1981. *The Expanding Circle: Ethics and Sociobiology*. New York: Farrar, Straus, and Giroux.

Skousen, Mark. 2001. *The Making of Modern Economics: The Lives and Ideas of the Great Thinkers*. New York: M. E. Sharpe.

Smith, Barry. 1994. *Austrian Philosophy: The Legacy of Franz Brentano*. LaSalle, IL: Open Court.

Smith, Craig. 2006. *Adam Smith's Political Philosophy: The Invisible Hand and Spontaneous Order*. London: Routledge.

Smith, Vernon. 2002. "Constructivist and Ecological Rationality in Economics." Stockholm: The Nobel Foundation.

Sowell, Thomas. 2002. *A Conflict of Visions: Ideological Origins of Political Struggles*. New York: Basic Books.

Sowell, Thomas. 2007. *Basic Economics: A Common Sense Guide to the Economy*, 3rd ed. New York: Basic Books, 2007.

Sunstein, Cass R. 1997. *Free Markets and Social Justice*. New York: Oxford University Press.

Sunstein, Cass R. 2008. *Infotopia: How Many Minds Produce Knowledge*. New York: Oxford University Press.

Sunstein, Cass R and Richard H. Thaler. 2008. *Nudge: Improving Decisions about Health, Wealth, and Happiness*. New Haven: Yale University Press.

Teichgraeber, Richard F. III. 1986. *"Free Trade" and Moral Philosophy: Rethinking the Sources of Adam Smith's "Wealth of Nations."* Durham, NC: Duke University Press.

Ubel, Peter A. 2009. *Free Market Madness: Why Human Nature Is at Odds with Economics—and Why It Matters*. Cambridge: Harvard Business Press.

Vanderbilt, Tom. 2008. *Traffic: Why We Drive the Way We Do (And What It Says About Us)*. New York: Vintage.

Vaughn, Karen I. 1998. *Austrian Economics in America: The Migration of a Tradition*. Cambridge: Cambridge University Press.

Veblen, Thorstein. 2008 (1899). *The Theory of the Leisure Class: An Economic Study of Institutions*. New York: Oxford University Press.

Viner, Jacob. 1928. "Adam Smith and Laissez Faire." In *Adam Smith, 1776–1926: Lectures to Commemorate the Sesquicentennial of the Publication of "The Wealth of Nations,"* John M. Clark et al., eds. Chicago: University of Chicago Press, 116–55.

Vivenza, Gloria. 2001. *Adam Smith and the Classics: The Classical Heritage in Adam Smith's Thought*. Oxford: Oxford University Press.

Way, K. Brad. March 2000. "Invisible Hands and the Success of Science." *Philosophy of Science* 67: 163–75.

Wilson, David Sloan. 2004. "The New Fable of the Bees: Multilevel Selection, Adaptive Societies, and the Concept of Self Interest." *Evolutionary Psychology and Economic Theory* 7: 201–220.

Wilson, Edward. O. 1998. *Consilience: The Unity of Knowledge*. New York: Vintage.

Wilson, Edward. 2004. *On Human Nature*, rev. ed. Cambridge: Harvard University Press.

Wilson, James Q. 1997. *The Moral Sense*. New York: Free Press.

Winch, Donald. 1978. *Adam Smith's Politics: An Essay in Historiographic Revision*. Cambridge: Cambridge University Press.

World Fact Book. 2010. Central Intelligence Agency. Available here: https://www.cia.gov/library/publications/the-world-factbook/index.html.

Young, Jeffrey T. 1997. *Economics as a Moral Science: The Political Economy of Adam Smith*. Gloucester, Edward Elgar.

Index